the knot

GUIDE TO

WEDDING

VOWS AND TRADITIONS

CARLEY RONEY

& the editors of The Knot

the knot

GUIDE TO

WEDDING

VOWS AND TRADITIONS

Readings, Rituals, Music,

Dances, Speeches, and Toasts

Clarkson Potter/Publishers
New York

All rights reserved.
Published in the United States by Clarkson Potter/Publishers,
an imprint of the Crown Publishing Group, a division of
Random House, Inc., New York
www.crownpublishing.com

CLARKSON POTTER is a trademark and POTTER with colophon
is a registered trademark of Random House, Inc.

Originally published in the United States by Broadway Books,
a division of Random House, Inc., New York, in 2000.

Library of Congress Cataloging-in-Publication Data

Roney, Carley.
   The Knot guide to wedding vows and traditions : readings, rituals, music, dances,
speeches, and toasts / Carley Roney—1st ed.
      p.   cm.
Includes bibliographical references and index.
1. Marriage customs and rites.   2. Wedding etiquette.   I. Title.
GT2690.R66   2000
392.5—dc21   00-030471

ISBN 978-0-7679-0248-9

Printed in the United States of America

Book design based on a design by Judith Stagnitto Abbate/Abbate Design
Cover design by Vela Tuohy
Cover photography by Elizabeth Messina, www.elizabethmessina.com

10 9 8 7 6 5 4 3 2 1

First Clarkson Potter/Publishers Edition

Readings

Contents

Rings and Other Rituals

Contents

PART FOUR

Programs and Quotes

Contents

Contents

ix

Contents

acknowledgments

I am very lucky to have an incredible team at The Knot to help me pull this together. Thanks to all who contributed, from research to reading to finding the images. A special thanks to Elisa Prainito, Tracy Guth, Julie Raimondi, and Maribeth Romslo.

The idea for this book came directly from the one million brides and grooms who visit TheKnot.com—"vows" and "music" are two of the most searched for words on the site! Their ideas and suggestions were invaluable in our researching and writing this book. So thank you all—particularly the couples who let us reproduce their original, and very moving, vows, photographs, and personal stories. (Thanks as well to their photographers for letting us use their photos. See their names in the photo credits in the back of the book.)

Many experts in the field gave this book depth. I'd particularly like to thank the celebrants who let us print the unique ceremony words that they have written, especially Bill Swetmon, Joyce Gioia, Joan Hawxhurst, the Reverends Irwin and Florence Schnurman, ordained lay clergyman Noah R. W. Saunders, and Dr. Tino Ballestaros. Thanks as well to the DJs and bandleaders—Steve McEwen, Reid Spears, and Ted Knight—who helped us put together the world's longest song list of first dance songs. Many of The Knot Editorial Advisory Board members also provided important expertise, particularly Harriette Cole and Peter Duchin.

Thank you to the team at Broadway Books for supporting this book so well.

I'd like to thank all the friends and colleagues and family who have shown brilliant insights and support along the way. Of special note are: my husband, David, and my daughter, Havana; my father, who introduced me to the brilliance of Rilke; my mother, the poet in the family;

xi

my father-in-law and stellar translator, Richard Liu; Jane Liu for her lullabies; a man of many musical genres (and impeccable research skills), Todd Spangler; my fellow cofounders Michael Wolfson and Rob Fassino; our talented creative director Catarina Tsang (who also generously allowed us to use her wedding photographs throughout the book); and, most of all, the millions of couples who rely on The Knot to help plan their weddings.

Acknowledgments

introduction

With all the details of planning a wedding reception, the ceremony is often the last thing you think about. But it is, of course, where the ultimate meaning lies—and where you have the most opportunity to express yourselves. Your guests should never mistake your wedding with the one that they went to last week. You have a golden opportunity to make statements throughout your wedding—about what you love about your relationship, about what is important to you both as you begin your life together. This book will help you to make your wedding as unique as you are. Here's what to remember as you plan:

Get swept away Even if you won't have readings at your wedding, spend a few evenings together indulging in the throbbing words about love and marriage that we've included here. They'll make you think, they'll make you cry, and they'll put into perspective any tensions the wedding planning may be causing you.

Put it in your own words No, you don't have to literally compose your entire ceremony. Just make sure you choose words that have meaning for you, and that you actually think about that meaning. Also, put away any preconceived notions you may have about religious words—they are often some of the most moving.

Dare to be different Your wedding should be rich with personality and culture. Think about all of the things that have meaning for you, and feel free to include them even if they are not completely wedding specific (even if that means having the words to a Patti Smith song on your invitation). What's most important is that these words, readings, and sayings have meaning for *you*. The worst thing that can happen is that people will ask and you'll have the chance to let them in on the secret. Don't be afraid to make people laugh!

If you find additional readings you love or a perfect first dance song that we have left out, let us know! Come to The Knot and submit your ideas (or find even more) at:

www.theknot.com/vows

www.theknot.com/readings

www.theknot.com/rituals

www.theknot.com/programs

www.theknot.com/quotes

www.theknot.com/music

www.theknot.com/toasts

Enjoy!

the knot

GUIDE TO

WEDDING

VOWS AND TRADITIONS

VOWS

While it's inevitable that most of the planning goes into the party, a wedding is ultimately about making a public promise. To be legally wed, all you really need to do is consent to marry each other before an authorized officiant: "Max, do you take Maria as your lawfully wedded wife?" "I do" (and vice versa) basically does it. But we're not going to let you off the hook that easily. Invest some time thinking through your commitment to each other. Whether you work with your own words or take up traditional religious vows, we want you to really mean what you are saying.

Traditional Religious Vows

Each religious faith has wedding traditions and practices, including marriage vows, that have been passed down through generations. The exact phrases used vary slightly from place to place and among different clergy—your officiant will most likely give you an outline that describes the entire ceremony as he or she generally performs it, as well as printed vows, which you may decide to say as written or use as a jumping-off point. Below you will find the common wordings and a few notes on the ceremony for each religious denomination. Don't be afraid to respectfully ask your priest, minister, or rabbi for a departure from the words they usually use.

Protestant Vows

There are many different types of Protestant churches, all with their own slightly different traditions and beliefs. There are also nondenominational Protestant churches that do not affiliate themselves with a larger religious organization. Talk to your chosen officiant about what vows he or she traditionally suggests. Below are guidelines for several denominations; you will find that many of them differ only slightly from one another. Most are based on the Protestant *Book of Common Prayer.*

Basic Protestant Vows

"I, ———, take thee, ———, to be my wedded wife/husband, to have and to hold, from this day forward, for better, for worse, for richer, for poorer, in sickness and in health, to love and to cherish, till death do us part, according to God's holy ordinance; and thereto I pledge thee my faith [or] pledge myself to you [or] plight thee my troth."

Lutheran Vows

"I take you, ———, to be my wife/husband from this day forward, to join with you and share all that is to come, and I promise to be faithful to you until death parts us."

"I, ———, take you, ———, to be my wife/husband, and these things I promise you: I will be faithful to you and honest with you; I will respect, trust, help, and care for you; I will share my life with you; I will forgive you as we have been forgiven; and I will try with you better to understand ourselves, the world, and God; through the best and the worst of what is to come, as long as we live."

Episcopal Vows

"———, wilt thou have this woman/man to be thy wedded wife/husband to live together after God's ordinance in the Holy Estate of matrimony? Wilt thou love her/him? Comfort her/him, honor and keep her/him, in sickness and in health, and forsaking all others keep thee only unto her/him as long as you both shall live?"

"In the name of God, I, ———, take you, ———, to be my wife/husband, to have and to hold from this day forward, for better, for worse, for richer, for poorer, in sickness and health, to love and to cherish, until we are parted by death. This is my solemn vow."

Methodist Vows

"Will you have this woman/man to be your wife/husband, to live together in a holy marriage? Will you love her/him, comfort her/him, honor and keep her/him in sickness and in health, and forsaking all others, be faithful to her/him as long as you both shall live?"

"In the name of God, I, ———, take you, ———, to be my wife/husband, to have and to hold from this day forward, for better, for worse, for richer, for poorer, in sickness and in health, to love and to cherish, until we are parted by death. This is my solemn vow."

Presbyterian Vows

"———, wilt thou have this woman/man to be thy wife/husband, and wilt thou pledge thy faith to her/him, in all love and honor, in all duty and service, in all faith and tenderness, to live with her/him, and cherish her/him, according to the ordinance of God, in the holy bond of marriage?"

"I, ———, take you, ———, to be my wedded wife/husband, and I do promise and covenant, before God and these witnesses, to be your loving and faithful husband/wife, in plenty and want, in joy and in sorrow, in sickness and in health, as long as we both shall live."

Baptist Vows

"Will you, ———, have ——— to be your wife/husband? Will you love her/him, comfort and keep her/him, and forsaking all others remain true to her/him, as long as you both shall live?"

"I, ———, take thee, ———, to be my wife/husband, and before God and these witnesses I promise to be a faithful and true husband/ wife."

Roman Catholic Vows

A traditional Catholic wedding ceremony takes place as part of a full Mass, but some couples choose a modified, shorter service. Whether you can do so may depend on the church you marry in and on your officiant.

"I, ———, take you, ———, to be my wife/husband. I promise to be true to you in good times and in bad, in sickness and in health. I will love you and honor you all the days of my life."

"I, ———, take you, ———, for my lawful wife/husband, to have and to hold from this day forward, for better, for worse, for richer, for poorer, in sickness and health, until death do us part."

What Was the Question?

You'll notice that some of the choices here are in the form of questions; others are statements. Your officiant may pose your vows to you as questions, and you would each answer "I do" or "I will," depending on how the question is phrased ("Do you take" or "Will you take"). Or, the question from your celebrant may be your declaration of consent—and then, in addition, you will say vows to each other.

Eastern Orthodox Vows

Eastern Orthodox wedding ceremonies (this includes Greek, Romanian, and Russian Orthodox) are rich with tradition, but often they do not include spoken vows. The rings are blessed and then exchanged between the couple three times, to represent the Holy Trinity of the Father, the

ASK CARLEY

Ceremony Itinerary

Q: What is the basic order of the ceremony from start to finish?

A: The vows are the center of most wedding ceremonies. Religious and cultural rituals differ, of course, but if you were to outline a standard service, it would look something like this:

Processional   The couple and wedding party enter the ceremony room or sanctuary, usually with accompanying music. The congregation generally stands for the bride's entrance.

Opening remarks   The officiant announces that everyone is there to celebrate the joining of the two of you in marriage; if it's a religious event he or she may offer a blessing to the congregation.

The "giving away"   If you will have your parents or friends "support you" in your marriage, or if you opt for the tradition of the bride's father giving her away, that happens now. This is also a time for your officiant and you to acknowledge your friends and family and the importance of their presence.

Statement of purpose/declaration of consent   The officiant asks the two of you whether you are each coming of your own free will to marry each other, and if you are prepared to do so. This is your public announcement—to the congregation gathered—of the vows you're about to take.

Exchange of vows   You promise to love each other as long as you both shall live! These are your personal words to each other.

Readings and rituals   These, as well as additional musical selections, may be incorporated throughout the service. Talk to your officiant and determine the order together, if possible.

Ring presentation/blessing/exchange   You give each other your wedding bands. The officiant may bless the rings as you do so.

Blessing/closing remarks from the officiant

Declaration of marriage   You are pronounced husband and wife! You kiss, gathered friends and family may applaud, and the recessional music begins.

Recessional   You leave the sanctuary as a married couple.

Son, and the Holy Spirit. The couple is also traditionally "crowned" with gold crowns connected to each other by a ribbon to symbolize the marriage connection. They are exchanged over the couple's heads three times to officially seal the union. After the bride and groom are led around the wedding platform three times, they are husband and wife.

However, in some denominations, including the Russian Orthodox Church, vows may be spoken aloud. An example:

> "I, _____, take you, _____, as my wedded wife/husband, and I promise you love, honor, and respect; to be faithful to you; and not to forsake you until death do us part. So help me God, one in the Holy Trinity, and all the saints."

Unitarian Vows

The Unitarian Universalist Church generally leaves service structure to individual ministers; your officiant may allow you significant freedom to create your own ceremony and vows. Suggested vows may borrow from traditional Christian versions:

> "I, _____, take you, _____, to be my wife/husband; to have and to hold from this day forward, for better, for worse, for richer, for poorer, in sickness and in health, to love and cherish always."

> "_____, will you take _____ to be your wife/husband; love, honor, and cherish her/him now and forevermore?"

Jewish Vows

There is no actual exchange of vows in a traditional Jewish ceremony; the covenant is said to be implicit in the ritual. Ceremony structure varies within the Orthodox, Conservative, and Reform synagogues, and also among individual rabbis. The marriage vow is customarily sealed when the groom places a ring on his bride's finger and says:

> "Behold, you are consecrated to me with this ring according to the laws of Moses and Israel."

However, today many Jewish couples opt for double-ring ceremonies, so the bride may also recite the traditional ring words, or a modified version. The traditional Seven Blessings, or *Sheva B'rachot* (see page 39), are also an integral part of Jewish wedding ceremonies; they are often recited by relatives and friends of the couple's choosing. And because many Jewish couples today do want to exchange spoken vows, they are now included in many Reform and Conservative ceremonies.

Reform

"Do you, ———, take ——— to be your wife/husband, promising to cherish and protect her/him, whether in good fortune or in adversity, and to seek together with her/him a life hallowed by the faith of Israel?"

Conservative

"Do you, ———, take ——— to be your lawfully wedded wife/husband, to love, to honor, and to cherish?"

Another version of nontraditional vows is a phrase from the biblical Song of Songs:

"*Ani leh-dodee veh-dodee lee*": "I am my beloved's, and my beloved is mine."

Muslim Vows

Muslim couples do not generally recite vows but rather listen to the words of the *imam,* or cleric (although any adult male Muslim may officiate), who speaks about the significance of the commitment of marriage and the couple's responsibilities toward each other and Allah. The bride and groom are asked three times if they accept each other in marriage according to the terms of their traditional marriage contract, or *Nikah.* Then they sign and the marriage is sealed; the gathered congregation may bless them.

However, some Muslim brides and grooms do choose to also exchange vows. Here is a common (quite traditional) recitation:

BRIDE: I, ———, offer you myself in marriage in accordance with the instructions of the Holy Koran and the Holy Prophet, peace and blessing be upon him. I pledge, in honesty and with sincerity, to be for you an obedient and faithful wife.

GROOM: I pledge, in honesty and sincerity, to be for you a faithful and helpful husband.

The ceremony might be augmented with readings from the Koran, the holy book of Islam. You might also consider a "honey ceremony," acknowledging the sharing of the "sweetness of life"; see page 88.

Hindu Vows

A traditional Hindu wedding ceremony is elaborate and complex, incorporating fifteen specific rituals. There are no "vows" in the Western sense, but the Seven Steps, or *Saptha Padhi,* around a flame (honoring the fire god Agni) spell out the promises the couple make to each other:

> "Let us take the first step to provide for our household a nourishing and pure diet, avoiding those foods injurious to healthy living.

> "Let us take the second step to develop physical, mental, and spiritual powers.

> "Let us take the third step to increase our wealth by righteous means and proper use.

> "Let us take the fourth step to acquire knowledge, happiness, and harmony by mutual love and trust.

> "Let us take the fifth step so that we are blessed with strong, virtuous, and heroic children.

> "Let us take the sixth step for self-restraint and longevity.

> "Finally, let us take the seventh step and be true companions and remain lifelong partners by this wedlock."

See page 87 for the pronouncement made after the couple have completed all seven steps (which also makes a beautiful reading for any type of wedding).

Quaker Vows

A Quaker wedding usually takes place during a regularly scheduled Meeting of Friends. The congregation and couple all worship silently until the bride and groom feel the time is right to stand and recite their vows to each other. There is no officiant—the Quaker belief is that only God can create the marriage bond. The words below are traditional, but after saying them couples often speak quite personally to each other.

"In the presence of God and these our friends I take thee, ————,
to be my husband/wife, promising with Divine assistance to be
unto thee a loving and faithful wife/husband so long as we both
shall live."

Buddhist Vows

Weddings in Buddhist countries are considered secular affairs, but the
couple usually also gets the blessing from monks at the local temple. For a
Western couple with no access to such a temple, there is no formal ceremony structure, but usually the couple erects a shrine with a Buddha
image, candles, and flowers. They light the candles, as well as incense,
and place the flowers around the Buddha as an offering. You may include
readings from the *Dhammapada,* a holy Buddhist book. Traditional
chants to Buddha include the Vandana, Tisarana, and Pancasila. You may
also choose to include the traditional Buddhist homily; see page 40.
Blessings from friends and family who are present (as well as the couple
bowing to their parents out of respect) are also inherent parts of the Buddhist wedding ceremony. There are no official vows; you may choose to
say original words to each other.

Interfaith and Nondenominational Vows

If the two of you are of different religions, you have several ceremony
options. You may choose to marry in just one of your churches or syna-
gogue (if it is allowed by your faith and officiant; ask your house of worship for details). You may decide to work with two officiants, one from
each faith; if this is the case you may say two sets of vows. Or, you may
choose a nondenominational or civil officiant, who will help you create
your own blended vows or allow you to write original vows (see the
Writing Your Own Vows section on page 16).

Many interfaith couples decide to express their religions in their ceremony's prayers, blessings, or rituals and reserve the vows as a place to talk
secularly about their feelings for each other. With this approach, your
possible vows are virtually unlimited.

Or, perhaps neither of you is religious, or you have other reasons to
want a nondogmatic ceremony. You don't have to forgo a spiritual element to your vows. The vows below, many courtesy of officiants who
marry couples of all spiritual and religious backgrounds, are appropriate
for interfaith and nondenominational couples alike.

So Little Has Changed!

If you haven't yet felt the power of tradition in wedding vows, check out these words from the Middle Ages—little has changed, except for Old English spelling, and, in many cases, the "obey" part:

"Wilte thou haue this woman to be thy wedde wife, to liue together after God-des ordeinuce in the holy estate of matrimonie? Wilt thou loue her, coumforte her, honor, and kepe her in sicknesse and in health? And forsaking all other kepe thee onely to her, so long as you bothe shall liue?"

The man shall aunswere: I will.

Then shall the priest saye to the woman:

"Wilt thou haue this man to be thy wedde houseband, to liue together after Goddes ordienaunce, in the holy estate of matrimonie? Wilt thou abey him and serue him, loue, honor, and kepe him in sicknesse, and in health? And for-saking all other kepe thee onely to him, so long as you bothe shall liue?"

The woman shall aunswere: I will.

A few updated versions that would be perfect for a nondenominational, inter-faith, or civil ceremony:

"_____, do you take _____ to be your wife/husband? Do you promise to love, honor, cherish, and protect her/him, forsaking all others and holding only unto her/him?"

"_____, do you take _____ to be your wife/husband? Do you promise to love, honor, cherish, and protect her/him, forsaking all others and holding only to her/him forevermore?"

From the Revs. Irwin and Florence Schnurman, interfaith ministers:

"I promise, _____, before family and friends, to commit my love to you; to respect your individuality; to be with you through life's changes; and to nurture and strengthen the love between us, as long as we both shall live."

From Joan Hawxhurst's book Interfaith Wedding Ceremonies:

"I love you. And I look forward to being your friend and compan-ion, your wife/husband and lover for life. I promise to love you and respect you; to stand by you and be faithful to you; to be open and honest with you; and to always work toward our mutual growth. I

I Take You—Who?

Exactly what do you say when you say your partner's name? Your officiant might have couples say the full name of their spouse-to-be ("Robert William Darnell"), or you may just use first names, or perhaps first and middle names. If you aren't having a superformal ceremony, use the name everyone is familiar with—for example, if everyone calls the groom Rex even though his real name is Richard. Unless the celebrant has a policy, this decision will probably be left to you. You actually just need to say the other person's name to make it clear whom you intend to marry!

promise this with the help of God, for the good times and the bad times, till death do us part."

"I, _____, cherish you, _____,
For being all that you are,
All that you are not,
And all that you can be.
Know that I am here for you,
And that your pain will be mine,
And your joy mine as well.
All I ask is you—your love—your trust—your caring.
I choose you to be my wife/husband."

"I take you to be my wife/husband, my friend, my love, and my lifelong companion: to share my life with yours. To build our dreams together, while allowing you to grow with your dreams; to support you through times of trouble, and rejoice with you in times of happiness; to treat you with respect, love, and loyalty through all the trials and triumphs of our lives together; and to give you all the love I can give my whole life long. This commitment is made in love, kept in faith, lived in hope, and eternally made new."

From Joyce Gioia, multifaith clergywoman:

"I, _____, choose you, _____, to be my wife/husband, my friend, my love, the mother/father of our children. I will be yours in plenty and in want, in sickness and in health, in failure and in triumph. I will cherish you and respect you, comfort you and encourage you, and together we shall live, freed and bound by our love."

"_____, do you now choose _____ to be your wife/husband, to share your life openly with her/him, to speak truthfully and lovingly to her/him, to accept her/him fully as she/he is and delight in who she/he is becoming, to respect her/his uniqueness, encourage her/his fulfillment, and compassionately support her/him through all the changes of your years together?"

"_____, will you have this woman/man to be your wife/husband, to live together in marriage? Will you love her/him and give her/him your respect? Will you comfort, honor, and keep her/him in sickness and in health, in joy and in sorrow, so long as love and life shall endure?"

"I, _____, take you, _____, as my husband/wife, to care for you and trust you, to cherish you and respect you, to forgive you and be forgiven by you. I will love you in good times and in bad, when we are together and when we are apart. I promise to be ever faithful, today and for all our tomorrows."

From Bill Swetmon, ordained nondenominational minister:

"————, will you take ———— to be your wife/husband? Do you commit yourself to her/his happiness and self-fulfillment as a person? Do you promise to love, honor, and trust her/him in sickness and in health, in adversity and prosperity, and to be true and loyal to her/him so long as you both shall live?"

"————, I promise to be faithful, supportive, and loyal and to give you my companionship and love throughout all the changes of our life. I vow to bring you happiness, and I will treasure you as my companion. I will celebrate the joys of life with you. I promise to support your dreams, and walk beside you offering courage and strength through all endeavors. From this day forward, I will be proud to be your wife/husband and your best friend."

"I choose you, ————, to be my wife/husband, as my friend and love. On this day I affirm the relationship we have enjoyed, looking to the future and to keep and strengthen it. I will be yours in plenty and in want, in sickness and in health, in failure and in triumph. Together, we will dream, and live as one while respecting one another, we will stumble but restore each other, we will share all things. I will cherish, comfort, and encourage you, be open with you, and stay with you as long as I shall live."

"I, ————, take you, ————, for my wedded wife/husband from this day forward, to have and to hold as equal partner in my life, to whom I give my deepest love and devotion. I humbly open my heart to you as a sanctuary of warmth and peace, where you may come and find a refuge of love and strength. I will love you enough to risk being hurt, trust you when I don't understand, weep with you in heartache, and celebrate life with you in joy. I will receive you as my equal throughout all of our days."

Other nondenominational options:

"I, ————, take you, ————, to be no other than yourself. Loving what I know of you, trusting what I do not yet know, I will respect your integrity and have faith in your abiding love for me, through all our years, and in all that life may bring us."

The following books focus on specific types of religious and cultural ceremonies and may further help you to design your ceremony—especially if you are joining multiple religions and/or backgrounds:

Jumping the Broom: The African-American Wedding Planner by Harriette Cole (Henry Holt, 1995)

The Nubian Wedding Book: Words and Rituals to Celebrate and Plan an African-American Wedding by Ingrid Sturgis (Three Rivers Press, 1998)

Going to the Chapel: From Traditional to African-Inspired, and Everything in Between—The Ultimate Wedding Guide to Today's Black Couple by the editors of Signature Bride (Putnam, 1999)

African-American Wedding Readings, edited by Tamara Nikuradse (Plume, 1999)

Wild Geese and Tea: An Asian-American Wedding Planner by Shu Shu Costa (Riverhead Books, 1998)

The New Jewish Wedding by Anita Diamant (Simon & Schuster, 2001)

Your Catholic Wedding: A Complete Plan-Book by Chris Aridas (Crossroad Publishing Co., 1997)

The Christian Wedding Planner by Ruth Muzzy and R. Kent Hughes (Tyndale House Publishing, 1991)

Interfaith Wedding Ceremonies: Samples and Sources edited by Joan C. Hawxhurst (Dovetail Publishing, 1997)

Celebrating Interfaith Marriages: Creating Your Jewish/Christian Ceremony by Devon A. Lerner (Owl Books, 1999)

The Protestant Wedding Sourcebook: A Complete Guide for Developing Your Own Service by Sidney F. Batts (Westminster John Knox Press, 1993)

A Humanist Wedding Service by Corliss Lamont (Prometheus Books, 1981)

The Traditional Irish Wedding by Bridget Haggerty (Irish Books & Media, 1999)

The Irish Wedding Book by Kim McGuire (Dufour Editions, Inc., 1995)

The Hindu Wedding Planner by Angirasa Muni (Sacred Books, 1999)

The Essential Guide to Lesbian and Gay Weddings by Tess Ayers and Paul Brown (Alyson Publications, 1999)

"_____, I take you as my wife/husband, with your faults and your strengths, as I offer myself to you with my faults and my strengths. I will help you when you need help, and turn to you when I need help. I choose you as the person with whom I will spend my life."

Ethical Humanist Vows

Members of Ethical Humanist societies are usually nontheistic—they believe in human ethics without the need of a religious authority. A humanist ceremony in its basic form focuses on the couple's relationship and the fact that they are making a public declaration of their commitment to be married. However, ministers are open to couples creating original ceremonies, and even including spiritual rituals—the officiant him- or herself simply will not mention God or recite any religious blessings. Below are some basic vows.

"_____, will you receive _____ as your lawfully wedded wife/husband? Will you share your life with her/him, hold your love firm, and dutifully care for her/him in all the varying circumstances of your life?"

"_____, will you have _____ as your wife/husband, to live together in marriage? Will you love her/him, comfort her/him, and honor her/him, in sickness and in health, in sorrow and in joy, as long as you both shall live?"

"I, _____, choose you, _____, to be my wife/husband. I will respect you, care for you, and grow with you, through good times and hard times, as your friend, companion, and partner, giving the best that I can, to fulfill our lives together."

Civil Vows

If you choose to marry in a civil service—at city hall, in a Las Vegas chapel, or simply with a judge or other public official as your officiant— you will probably use a very simple, basic vow. If you plan somewhat in advance, however, your officiant will probably allow you to write your own vows or recite words of your own choosing. The following are basic civil vows to start with:

"_____, do you take _____ as your lawfully wedded wife/husband?"

If you're marrying again, it doesn't have to affect your vows, but you may decide that you want to do something different this time. For example, if you exchanged traditional Protestant vows at your first wedding, you could write original words this time. Discuss it with your partner and make the decision together.

"_____, do you take _____ to be your legal wedded wife/husband, to have and to hold from this day forward?"

"_____, I take you to be my lawfully wedded wife/husband. Before these witnesses I vow to love you and care for you for as long as we both shall live."

Writing Your Own Vows

There's something very meaningful about repeating the vows that thousands of brides and grooms before you have used. But if you aren't constrained for religious reasons to stick with standard vows, we strongly suggest you take a crack at crafting your own. Putting your promises on

---

Make a Vow Date

Go out to dinner or set aside an evening at home to take some time to talk about the important days, events, and turning points in your relationship. Be sure to have notepads and pens handy and discuss the following:

- When did you fall in love? Why?

- When did you each say "I love you" for the first time?

- What qualities do you most admire in each other?

- What does your partner bring out in you?

- What ways are you alike? Different? How do you complement each other?

- Why did you decide to get married?

- What hard times have you gone through together? What have you supported each other through?

- Did you ever break up or almost break up? What got you back together or made you stay together?

- What do you have together that you don't have apart?

- What challenges do you envision in your future? What do you want to accomplish together?

- What, in your view, is the most important part of marriage?

You may or may not be able to incorporate some of this into your vows—but either way, you will have one romantic date!

paper is an emotional, eye-opening, and often extremely memorable experience. Even if you end up with very traditional-sounding words, it will be worth the trip—we promise.

Writers' Guidelines

We can't say this enough: Start early! Don't leave writing your vows until the day before. You'll be much too nervous, excited, and rattled to give them the time and thought they deserve. Give yourselves at least a month or two, or work on your vows in that pocket of time after you've set up all your major wedding vendors and before you have to start thinking about details. This should be done in a relaxed, not rushed, frame of mind. Here are some tips on the process:

- Examine traditional religious vows—your own, if you practice a certain faith, but others, as well—to see what strikes a chord with you. You can incorporate them into the original words you write, or at least use them as a jumping-off point.

- Borrow freely from poetry, love stories, religious and spiritual texts—even from romantic movies. Jot down words and phrases that capture your feelings. Widely recognized works ring true for a reason. See Part 2, Readings (page 29), for inspiration.

- Before you begin, talk about what marriage means to each of you. Discuss what you expect from each other and the relationship; how you each define words like *respect, cherish, love, support, commit,* and *promise,* and how you would prioritize those things; and how you envision yourselves growing older together. Not only will this help you to focus on what kind of vows you want to write—it's good for you!

- Decide whether you will each write your vows separately. If you do, you'll probably run them by each other before the wedding, though saving the words until the wedding day can make for quite an emotional moment. Some couples write a mutual vow that they will both take, as you would with traditional vows.

- Once you've done all your research—talking to each other and looking at traditional vows and other written words of love—start writing! Try to get a first draft together at least two to three weeks before the wedding.

- Your vows can be clever and light, but they should acknowledge the seriousness of the commitment you're about to make. If it's okay with your officiant, it's fine to throw in a humorous comment—"I promise to love you, adore you, and let you watch *Monday Night Football*"—but don't make the whole thing a joke.

- Don't make your vows so personal that they're cryptic—or embarrassing! You've invited your family and friends to witness your vows in order to make your bond public, so be sure everyone feels included in the moment.

- Don't make them too long—one minute or so is longer than it sounds! Your vows are the most important element of your ceremony, but that doesn't mean they should go on for hours. Save some thoughts for toasting at the reception—and for the wedding night. Your vows should get at the heart of what marrying this person means to you; pick the most important points and make them well.

- Ask your officiant if he or she will want to approve your vows before the big day. If you're having a religious ceremony the officiant most definitely will. She or he may raise faith-based questions—or even objections to some of your wording—but may also contribute interesting thoughts or quotes for you to consider.

- Have a final version at least two days before your wedding. Practice out loud. These are words meant to be heard by an audience, so be sure they sound good when spoken. Avoid tongue twisters and watch out for superlong sentences; you don't want to get out of breath.

- Decide whether you'll memorize your words. Most officiants give this idea the thumbs-down—you'll probably be so nervous or emotional that your mind will go blank! Either read them to each other or have the officiant say them for you to repeat.

- Make sure your guests will be able to hear you! Consider microphones (tiny lavaliers) if your wedding is large or will be held outside. If your guests can't understand, they'll disconnect. You may want to print your vows in your program, so that even if those gathered can't hear every word, they can still follow along.

Real Couples' Vows

Below are the vows some recent Knot brides and grooms used in their weddings. Let them inspire you in writing yours. (We've printed one partner's words to the other; unless otherwise noted, the other person then repeated the same words.)

Jolene and Rodney looked at sample vows in many books and pieced together the words that they felt said what they wanted to say.

"Jolene, will you have Rodney as your wedded husband, to live together in the covenant of faith, hope, and love? Will you listen to his deepest thoughts, be tenderhearted, kind, and wise in your daily care of him, and stand faithfully at his side in sickness and health? Choosing him above all others, will you undertake to care for his well-being of mind, body, and spirit, as long as you both shall live?" [Officiant repeated to Rodney; both said "I will."]

"I, Jolene, take you, Rodney, from this day forward to be my husband. I promise always to love you, to honor you, to adore you. To laugh with you in the good times, to struggle with you in the bad, to stand by your side and cherish you always."

Dana and Joe chose to use traditional vows, but they added a slightly personal touch that really spoke to the spirit of their relationship.

"With this ring, in the presence of God, I, Dana, take you, Joseph, to be my husband. I promise to be true to you in good times and in bad, in sickness and in health. I will love you and honor you, make you laugh, wipe your tears, and hold your hand all the days of my life."

Kristen and Ken found it easy to put together the words they wanted to say to each other; they wrote these vows in less than five minutes.

"I take you, Kristen, as my wife. I promise to love and cherish you, to grow with you, and to have faith in our journey together through all the changes that will come. Will you let me share my life and all that I am with you?"

Dawn and David wrote vows that were said in conjunction with the traditional ones.

The couple's words:

"To my dearest Dawn/David,
Today is the day I give all of me to all of you.

On this day, I promise to support you mentally,
  emotionally, and spiritually,
so that we may continually grow together as one.

Renewing Your Vows

If you opted for a church wedding to make your parents happy, but what you really wanted was to exchange spiritual vows on a mountaintop—or if you had a small civil ceremony ten years ago and now want a big, religious wedding—consider renewing your vows. An anniversary is a wonderful time to make your promises to each other once again. You can either have a small, intimate ceremony with just the two of you and your families (or just the two of you), or you can, throw a big wedding celebration with all of your family and friends. It may be especially meaningful to you to say the exact same vows again—or you might write new words that represent your relationship as it is now.

Vows

On this day, I promise to be your confidant(e),
so that your heart may always be open to me.

On this day, I promise to offer you comfort in bad times,
so that we may be stronger in hours of need.

On this day, I promise to rejoice with you in good times,
so that we may know the blessing of sharing happiness.

Above all, on this day, I thank you for choosing me to love,
    support, comfort, and confide in,
and I thank God for allowing me to know the love that is
    within, and that is . . . you."

From the minister:

"I, David/Dawn, take you, Dawn/David,
to be my lawfully wedded wife/husband,
to come to this life filled with caring, honesty, and mutual
    respect.
I vow to love, honor, and cherish you
through all the changes of our lives,
for as long as we both shall live."

Vows adapted from Jumping the Broom: The African-American Wedding Planner
by Harriette Cole (Henry Holt, 1995) and The Nubian Wedding Book: Words and
Rituals to Celebrate and Plan an African-American Wedding *by Ingrid Sturgis
(Three Rivers Press, 1998)*

*Sara and Derek borrowed some of their words from vows they researched; other
sections were added to be more personal and meaningful. Since they were long,
the bride and groom said them together. "Derek cried through the whole
thing," Sara says.*

"Today, I join my life to yours.
From this day on, I will be your partner and companion,
for you are my dearest love and my best friend.
I look forward to the joy we will find
in each other's separate successes,
as well as our shared ones;
I welcome the challenge of whatever
obstacles we encounter,
for I know that whatever we face,
we face it together.
Because your happiness is vital to me,
I will help you to grow as an individual.

Because you deserve no less than the best of me,
I will also strive to be more fully myself.
I pledge that I will listen to you when you speak,
encourage you in times of doubt,
comfort you in times of sorrow,
and be your refuge of strength in times of uncertainty.
I will be faithful to you all of my days,
will be honest with you always,
and will cherish and adore you every moment of my life.
This is my solemn vow."

Vasia said the following vow to her husband, Lawrence, on their wedding day. As for Lawrence, "He did a freestyle verse the morning of the wedding that turned out to be a sermon," Vasia says. "I'd have to review the videotape a billion times to get everything correct, verbatim!"

"Lawrence, Helen Keller has taught me that 'the best and most beautiful things in the world cannot be seen or even touched; they must be felt with the heart.' Now that we are beyond the romantic phase that every new couple endures, and our consciousness is no longer impaired, I see things clearly with both my heart *and* my head.

ASK CARLEY
Family Vows

Q: How can we get our children involved in the ceremony?

A: Your kids are an important part of your new family—let them know it during your ceremony. Here are some great ways to make them feel a part of things:

- Do a family ring exchange. You and your partner give each other rings, and then the two of you present rings to the kids.

- Or, give each child another piece of jewelry, like a wristwatch, cuff links, or a bracelet, after the two of you have exchanged vows and rings.

- Present kids with family medallions, which take the shape of three joined circles—two for the couple and the third representing the child.

- Have the kids' "new" parent say vows to the children. An example:

  "———, I promise to accept and love you as my own and to protect and love you all of my life. I will to do my best to guide and support you." (You may add your own personal words—a few additional sentences—here.)

TINA AND KEN

August 29
Lincoln, Massachusetts

THE PRESENCE OF FRIENDS AND FAMILY was paramount to Tina and Ken, and it was perfectly epitomized in a communal blessing of the rings. "We passed our rings around and asked everyone to say a silent prayer or blessing as they held them in their hands," Tina says. The unique ritual actually evolved from the music the couple chose: "We had a classical vocalist and guitarist and a favorite piece we wanted them to play," explains the bride. "But we didn't want our guests to have to sit and stare at us! So our minister helped us plan something that was more interactive." The rings, tied together with straw in keeping with the setting (in a meadow by a pond), were passed at the beginning of the ceremony, after the introductory address. "The timing worked well; the rings came back to us right before we said our vows," Tina said.

"Our relationship is ever growing and evolving, as any relationship striving for success will do. You and I are imperfect human beings in an imperfect world. Therefore, as much as society would like us to believe that love conquers all, you and I both know that that is a whimsical myth. With the world running at such a fast pace, there can be no marriage today without a conscious effort for tomorrow. Marriage is not self-sustaining. Marriage is not a nine-to-five job, but rather a corporation that requires nonstop nurturing. If we fail to labor in the vineyard, there will be no reward.

"Our union has been one of mind, heart, and spirit. Today we will be joined in body, making our union complete. On this day I make a covenant with you and the Creator. I know that together, with God as our center, we can reach any goal we envision.

"I, Vashia, take you, Lawrence, to be my husband, loving you in your growing and becoming. I will honor your goals and your dreams and help you to fulfill them. I shall stand by you in every success and failure you encounter. I will love you whether you are near or far, when you are at your best or at your worst; in times of joy and in times of sorrow. I say these things knowing that God is in the midst of them all. Lawrence, I am your wife from this day forward. I will walk with you all the days of my life."

Jason and Nancy chose to write questions for their minister to ask each of them as well as vows to say to each other.

MINISTER: Do you, Jason, take Nancy as your wife, joining with her today in spirit, offering your friendship and loving care? Do you promise to honor her growth and freedom as well as your own, to cherish and respect her, to love and embrace her in times of challenge as well as times of joy? If so, now say, "I do."

JASON: Nancy, I choose you to be my partner in love and in life. I promise to nurture you—body, mind, and spirit. I will laugh and cry with you. I will always stand by you. Will you be my wife? (*Nancy replies.*)

MINISTER: Do you, Nancy, take Jason as your husband, joining with him today in spirit? Do you promise to care for him and share with him, to love him and learn from him, to laugh with him and listen to him? To grow with him? If so, now say, "I do."

NANCY: Jason, I love and respect you. I will comfort, support, and uplift you. I will honor your spirit for the rest of my days. Will you be my husband? (*Jason replies.*)

For their vows, Robin and Adam read the text of their ketubah, *the Jewish marriage contract, which they wrote based on the traditional model.*

"Be my wife/husband according to the tradition of Moses and the people of Israel. I take you to be mine in love and friendship. I will nourish, respect, and support you with integrity and faithfulness. We stand under the *huppah* before family and friends to make a mutual covenant, becoming partners in marriage—loving and supportive companions in life. Together we will build a home, part of the community of Israel, guided by a reverence for the Divine and the laws, traditions, and ethics of our people. The symbols and rituals we cherish will forge a link to our heritage, a bond strengthened by learning, involvement, and acts of loving kindness.

"Should we be blessed to raise children, we will give them a loving home and share with them a deep appreciation for our history and culture. We will be linked eternally to the history of our ancestors and the future of the Jewish people. We, as beloveds and friends, will develop our lives individually and together, responsible to and for each other. We will fill our lives with laughter and affection. We will encourage each other's music and writing. Together, we will support each other's intellectual, emotional, spiritual, and creative fulfillment.

"We declare that just as this is a permanent joining of our two lives, so it also constitutes a joining of material substance and worth. Through marriage we assume the responsibility to support each other and our family. If we should part, we promise to act with concern and compassion for the physical, economic, and emotional needs of each other and those whose lives are intertwined with ours. Joyfully we enter into this covenant of marriage and we solemnly accept its obligations. It is valid and binding."

Katherine and Kenneth wrote their own shared vows, as well as separate passages, to express their individual feelings to each other.

"I, Kenneth/Katherine, take you, Katherine/Kenneth, to be my lawful wedded wife/husband, to be my friend, my lover, and the mother/father of my children. I will be yours in times of plenty and in times of want, in times of sickness and in times of health, in times of joy and in times of sorrow, in times of failure and in times of triumph. I promise to cherish and respect you, to care for and protect you, to comfort and encourage you, and stay with you, for all eternity."

KENNETH: Although we have lived together, it has not been enough. Today I choose to make a deeper commitment to you. It is my way of telling you that our experiences together have been so good that I want them to continue for the rest of my life. I loved you before this ceremony and I love you more because of it. You are everything I ever hoped to find in a partner. I want to spend the rest of my life with you and I promise to be the best person I can be so that our lifetime together will be one of happiness and growth.

KATHERINE: I do not ask you to fulfill all my dreams. I only ask that you share them with me and allow me to share your dreams with you. I promise to do all in my power to keep our love as fresh and strong as it is today. I promise to be a true and loyal friend to you. I will try to be worthy of your love and trust. I will love you for today and for all of our tomorrows. From this day forward, I will walk beside you.

Kim and Tom's original vows focused on friendship.

"Kim/Tom, you are my best friend and the one I want to share my life with. I will love you forever, and under all circumstances. I will stand by you always. I will have faith in you and encourage you in everything you do. I will be here to listen to you, to laugh with you, and to hold you. I will work with you as we build a life together, and I will support you as you live your own independent life. I will strive every day to make our relationship stronger. I will be your friend, your love, and your partner for all the days of our lives."

For more ideas on vows or to submit your own,
visit www.theknot.com/vows.

NOTES

readings

ove—along with birth and death—is probably the most written about topic in human history. Writers through the centuries have philosophized about, pondered over, raged against, and swooned before the idea of love, and they have done so in so many unique, beautiful, and inspiring ways that you'll have countless choices for wedding readings. From Scripture to Shakespeare to the poetry of E. E. Cummings or Pablo Neruda, chances are some scribe has perfectly articulated the feelings you want to express on your wedding day.

Becoming Well-Read

But with all the wonderful words of the world's greatest scribes out there at your disposal, how do you choose the ones that mean the most to the two of you? Begin by asking yourselves some questions.

What to Select?

* If you feel an affinity for a certain poet, if you've never forgotten the passage about Cathy and Heathcliff's love in *Wuthering Heights* (which you first read in high school), or if your fiancé presented you with a copy of Shakespeare's *Sonnets* on your first Christmas together, including such readings in your ceremony is priceless.

* If you're having a religious ceremony, there may be certain requirements about or restrictions on what can be read. Your officiant may give you a list of approved pieces of Scripture to choose from.

* If you're looking for a way to honor a deceased or absent parent, reading a favorite poem or piece of prose or Scripture is

appropriate. Reading excerpts of an old letter written during their life is another moving option.

- Readings are a wonderful way to place your wedding in a period. If you're planning a celebration with a medieval or Victorian flair, choose poems and passages from those times.

- Feel free to use ethnic or cultural readings that don't necessarily reflect your backgrounds—what's important is that the words resonate for you. Do explain the reading's source in the program or introduction: e.g., "an Aztec marriage poem."

- If you find many very short passages that you really like, consider having multiple readers recite them one after the other, with each person being introduced before he reads (like the Jewish Seven Blessings; see page 39).

- A song is just a poem put to music—your favorite lyrics may make a great selection.

- Do you have a piece you really adore, but don't trust anyone else to perform as brilliantly as you would? Be a reader yourself, or encourage your partner to read. Or read to each other and surprise your new spouse with your selection.

- Sometimes couples choose a reader but leave the choice of the reading up to her. Make sure your readers clear their selections with your officiant to avoid any faux pas.

- You or your partner may be moved to write something original for the ceremony—a poem, perhaps. Either read it yourself, or ask a close friend or relative to do so.

- Keep in mind that passages from wedding readings can also be used in toasts, or as quotes to grace your invitations or programs. (See page 97 for more ideas.)

Who Reads?

- You may want to choose friends and relatives whom you want to involve in the ceremony in some way, but who are not in the wedding party. Parents and grandparents can read as well. Ask readers well ahead of time to participate—at least four months before the wedding—and give them a copy of what they'll be reading, so they can practice. And do be gracious if they decline. Public speaking *is* the number one fear of most Americans!

- You may want to ask your officiant to introduce each reader as her cue ("And now Elizabeth, the bride's friend, will read a passage from . . ."). Not only will they not have the extra stress of worrying about when it's time to stand up, but all your guests will know each person's significance to you.

- People tend to get nervous and start speaking too quickly. Reassure your readers that there is plenty of time for them to read, so they should try to speak slowly and clearly (and remember to breathe!).

- Make sure each reader gives the title and author (and significance, if appropriate) of the piece before starting to read. Also put this info in your ceremony program, if you'll have one.

- Some of the readings listed here or that you'll find elsewhere may have a specific gender bent—i.e., they may extol the beauty of a lady from a man's point of view. You'll want to make sure that something like that is read by an appropriate person—a male reader, if not the groom himself.

How's It Done?

- Readings are usually interspersed throughout the ceremony. You might plan one right after the greeting, another after your vows but before the ring exchange, and one to close the ceremony, before the recessional music. Talk to your officiant about exactly how things will flow; he or she may leave it up to you, or may have a specifc ceremony order he or she usually follows.

- Depending on how large your wedding is, readers may be able to remain standing at their seat to read, or they may need to come up to the stage or altar and read into a microphone. (They should all be invited to the rehearsal to go over the ceremony order and their place in it.)

- There's no set time limit on readings, but in the interest of short attention spans, make sure they're not too long. A simple poem can be read in less than a minute in most cases; a piece of prose may take several more. (You might want to excerpt the most significant passages from a longer piece instead of having someone read the entire thing.) Four or five minutes tops is probably more than enough time for the readers to express the sentiment for which you chose the piece.

- Have copies of the readings to hand out if you aren't having a program. Wrapped in a nice way, these make a great favor. For example, you could have them printed on nice parchment paper, rolled into a scroll, and tied with a ribbon. Place them at your guests' place settings or at least set them out in baskets for guests to take as they leave the ceremony site.

Traditional Religious Readings

Religious texts are the source of some of the most beautiful verses on the subject of marriage. Even if you are having a secular or nontraditional ceremony, consider using any of the passages below.

Scripture

Please note that couples marrying in the Catholic Church should choose their readings from a prescribed list, which does not include all the selections listed below, but does include additional texts.

Old Testament

The LORD God said: "It is not good for the man to be alone. I will make a suitable partner for him." So the LORD God formed out of the ground various wild animals and various birds of the air, and he brought them to the man to see what he would call them; whatever the man called each of them would be its name. The man gave names to all the cattle, all the birds of the air, and all the wild animals; but none proved to be the suitable partner for the man.

So the LORD God cast a deep sleep on the man, and while he was asleep, he took out one of his ribs and closed up the place with flesh. The LORD God then built up into a woman the rib that he had taken from the man. When he brought her to the man, the man said:

"This one, at last, is bone of my bones
and flesh of my flesh;
This one shall be called 'woman,'
for out of 'her man' this one has been taken."

That is why a man leaves his father and mother and clings to his wife, and the two of them become one body.

—*Genesis 2:18–24*

Ruth said, "Do not ask me to abandon or forsake you! for wherever you go I will go, wherever you lodge I will lodge, your people shall be my people, your God my God. Wherever you die I will die, and there be buried. May the LORD do so and so to me, and more besides, if aught but death separates me from you!"

—*Ruth 1:16–17*

Two are better than one: they get a good wage for their labor. If the one falls, the other will lift up his companion. Woe to the solitary man! For if he should fall, he has no one to lift him up. So also, if two sleep together, they keep each other warm. How can one alone keep warm? Where a lone man may be overcome, two together can resist. A three-ply cord is not easily broken.

—*Ecclesiastes 4:9–12*

Go, eat your bread with joy and drink your wine with a merry heart, because it is now that God favors your works. At all times let your garments be white, and spare not the perfume for your head. Enjoy life with the wife whom you love, all the days of the fleeting life that is granted you under the sun. This is your lot in life, for the toil of your labors under the sun.

—*Ecclesiastes 9:7–9*

Set me as a seal on your heart,
    as a seal on your arm;
For stern as death is love,
    relentless as the nether world is devotion;
    its flames are a blazing fire.
Deep waters cannot quench love,
    nor floods sweep it away.
Were one to offer all he owns to purchase love,
    he would be roundly mocked.

—*Song of Songs (Song of Solomon) 8:6–7*

I rejoice heartily in the LORD,
    in my God is the joy of my soul;
For he has clothed me with a robe of salvation,
    and wrapped me in a mantle of justice,
Like a bridegroom adorned with a diadem,
    like a bride bedecked with her jewels.
As the earth brings forth its plants,
    and a garden makes its growth spring up,
So will the LORD GOD make justice and praise
    spring up before all the nations.

For Zion's sake I will not be silent,
  for Jerusalem's sake I will not be quiet,
Until her vindication shines forth like the dawn
  and her victory like a burning torch.
Nations shall behold your vindication,
  and all kings your glory;
You shall be called by a new name
  pronounced by the mouth of the LORD.
You shall be a glorious crown in the hand of the LORD,
  a royal diadem held by your God.
No more shall men called you "Forsaken,"
  or your land "Desolate,"
But you shall be called "My Delight,"
  and your land "Espoused."
For the LORD delights in you,
  and makes your land his spouse.
As a young man marries a virgin,
  your Builder shall marry you;
And as a bridegroom rejoices in his bride
  so shall your God rejoice in you.

  —*Isaiah 61:10–62:5*

So I will allure her;
  I will lead her into the desert
  and speak to her heart.
From there I will give her the vineyards she had,
  and the valley of Achor as a door of hope.
She shall respond there are in the days of her youth,
  when she came up from the land of Egypt.
  On that day, says the LORD,
She shall call me "My husband."

I will espouse you to me forever:
  I will espouse you in right and in justice,
  in love and in mercy;
I will espouse you in fidelity,
  and you shall know the LORD.

  —*Hosea 2:14–16; 19–20*

New Testament

This is my commandment:
love one another
as I have loved you.

There is no greater love than this:
to lay down one's life for one's friends.

It was not you who chose me,
it was I who chose you
to go forth and bear fruit.
Your fruit must endure,
so that all you ask the Father in my name
he will give you.
The command I give you is this,
that you love one another.

—John 15:12–13; 16–17

Your love must be sincere. Detest what is evil, cling to what is good. Love one another with the affection of brothers. Anticipate each other in showing respect. Do not grow slack but be fervent in spirit; he whom you serve is the LORD. Rejoice in hope, be patient under trial, persevere in prayer. Look on the needs of the saints as your own; be generous in offering hospitality. Bless your persecutors; bless and do not curse them. Rejoice with those who rejoice, weep with those who weep. Have the same attitude toward all. Put away ambitious thoughts and associate with those who are lowly. Do not be wise in your own estimation. Never repay injury with injury. See that your conduct is honorable in the eyes of all. If possible, live peaceably with everyone.

—Romans 12:9–18

If I speak with human tongues and angelic as well, but do not have love, I am a noisy gong, a clanging cymbal. If I have the gift of prophecy, and, with full knowledge, comprehend all mysteries, if I have faith great enough to move mountains, but have not love, I am nothing. If I give everything I have to feed the poor and hand over my body to be burned, but have not love, I gain nothing.

Love is patient; love is kind. Love is not jealous, it does not put on airs, it is not snobbish. Love is never rude, it is not self-seeking, it is not prone to anger; neither does it brood over injuries. Love does not rejoice in what is wrong but rejoices with the truth. There is no limit to love's forbearance, to its trust, its hope, its power to endure.

Love never fails. Prophecies will cease, tongues will be silent, knowledge will pass away. . . . There are in the end three things that last: faith, hope, and love, and the greatest of these is love.

—1 Corinthians 13:1–8; 13

That is why I kneel before the Father from whom every family in heaven and on earth takes its name; and I pray that he will bestow on you gifts in keeping with the riches of his glory. May he strengthen you inwardly through the working of his Spirit. May Christ dwell in your hearts through faith, and may charity be the root and foundation of your life. Thus you will be able to grasp fully, and with all the holy ones, the breadth and length and height and depth of Christ's love, and experience this love which surpasses all knowledge, so that you may attain to the fullness of God himself.

—*Ephesians 3:14–19*

I plead with you then, as a prisoner for the LORD, to live a life worthy of the calling you have received, with perfect humility, meekness, and patience, bearing with one another lovingly. Make every effort to preserve the unity which has the Spirit as its origin and peace as its blinding force. There is but one body and one Spirit, just as there is but one hope given all of you by your call. . . . Be imitators of God as his dear children. Follow the way of love, even as Christ loved you. He gave himself for us as an offering to God, a gift of pleasing fragrance.

—*Ephesians 4:1–4; 5:1–2*

Because you are God's chosen ones, holy and beloved, clothe yourselves with heartfelt mercy, with kindness, humility, meekness, and patience. Bear with one another; forgive whatever grievances you have against one another. Forgive as the LORD has forgiven you. Over all these virtues put on love, which binds the rest together and makes them perfect. Christ's peace must reign in your hearts, since as members of the one body you have been called to that peace. Dedicate yourselves to thankfulness. Let the word of Christ, rich as it is, dwell in you. In wisdom made perfect, instruct and admonish one another. Sing gratefully to God from your hearts in psalms, hymns, and inspired songs. Whatever you do, whether in speech or in action, do it in the name of the Lord Jesus. Give thanks to God the Father through him.

—*Colossians 3:12–17*

Let us love in deed and truth
and not merely talk about it.
This is our way of knowing we are committed to the truth
and are at peace before him
no matter what our consciences may charge us with;
for God is greater than our hearts

and all is known to him.
Beloved,
if our consciences have nothing to charge us with,
we can be sure that God is with us
and that we will receive at his hands
whatever we ask.
Why? Because we are keeping his commandments
and doing what is pleasing in his sight.
His commandment is this:
we are to believe in the name of his Son, Jesus Christ,
and are to love one another as he commanded us.
Those who keep his commandments remain in him
and he in them.
And this is how we know that he remains in us:
from the Spirit that he gave us.

—*1 John 3:18–24*

Beloved,
let us love one another
because love is of God;
everyone who loves is begotten of God
and has knowledge of God.
The man without love has known nothing of God,
for God is love.
God's love was revealed in our midst in this way:
he sent his only Son to the world
that we might have life through him.
Love, then, consists in this:
not that we have loved God,
but that he has loved us
and has sent his Son as an offering for our sins.
Beloved,
if God has loved us so,
we must have the same love for one another.
No one has ever seen God.
Yet if we love one another
God dwells in us,
and his love is brought to perfection in us.

We have come to know and to believe
in the love God has for us.
God is love,
and he who abides in love

Responsorial Psalms

Christian ceremonies usually include a responsorial psalm; you may be able to have close friends and relatives contribute by leading the response (usually the first line of the psalm or another well-known line in it) or reciting the verses, or your officiant may have a church official do so. Here are a few possibilities; look at the Book of Psalms or talk to your officiant for more ideas.

I

I will bless the LORD at all times;
    his praise shall be ever in my mouth.
Let my soul glory in the LORD;
    the lowly will hear me and be glad.
Glorify the LORD with me,
    let us together extol his name.

II

I sought the LORD, and he answered me
    and delivered me from all my fears.
Look to him that you may be radiant with joy,
    and your faces may not blush with shame.

III

Come, children, hear me;
    I will teach you the fear of the LORD.
Which of you desires life,
    and takes delight in prosperous days?
Keep your tongue from evil
    and your lips from speaking guile;
Turn from evil, and do good;
    seek peace, and follow after it.
The LORD has eyes for the just,
    and ears for their cry.
The LORD confronts the evildoers,
    to destroy remembrance of them from the earth.
When the just cry out, the LORD hears them,
    and from all their distress he rescues them.
      —from Psalm 34

Sing joyfully to the LORD, all you lands;
    serve the LORD with gladness;
    come before him with joyful song.
Know that the LORD is God;
    he made us, his we are;
    his people, the flock he tends.
Enter his gates with thanksgiving,
    his courts with praise;
Give thanks to him; bless his name, for he is good:

the LORD, whose kindness endures forever,
    and his faithfulness, to all generations.
      —Psalm 100

I

Give thanks to the LORD, for he is good,
    for his mercy endures forever;
Give thanks to the God of gods,
    for his mercy endures forever;
Give thanks to the LORD of lords,
    for his mercy endures forever;

II

Who alone does great wonders,
    for his mercy endures forever;
Who made the heavens in wisdom,
    for his mercy endures forever;
Who spread out the earth upon the waters,
    for his mercy endures forever;
Who made the great lights,
    for his mercy endures forever;
The sun to rule over the day,
    for his mercy endures forever;
The moon and the stars to rule over the night,
    for his mercy endures forever.
      —from Psalm 136

Praise the LORD in his sanctuary,
    praise him in the firmament of his strength.
Praise him for his mighty deeds,
    praise him for his sovereign majesty.
Praise him with the blast of the trumpet,
    praise him with lyre and harp,
Praise him with timbrel and dance,
    praise him with strings and pipe.
Praise him with sounding cymbals,
    praise him with clanging cymbals.
Let everything that has breath
    praise the LORD! Alleluia.
      —Psalm 150

abides in God,
and God in him.

Love has no room for fear;
rather, perfect love casts out all fear.
And since fear has to do with punishment,
love is not yet perfect in one who is afraid.
We, for our part, love
because he first loved us.

—*1 John 4:7–12; 16; 18–19*

The Jewish Seven Blessings (*Sheva B'rachot*)

The seven Jewish wedding blessings praise God for creating the fruit of
the vine (wine); humankind; man and woman; the miracle of childbirth;
bringing the bride and groom together like the first couple, Adam and
Eve; the couple's joy and the hope for a future filled with their joy, and
the voices of their children. Usually couples choose seven relatives and
friends to recite them.

We have chosen an egalitarian translation of the seven blessings. There
are many different versions; please consult your rabbi regarding the best
translation to use in your ceremony.

Blessed are You, Adonai our God, Source of the universe, who created the fruit of the vine, symbol of joy.

Blessed are You, Adonai our God, Source of the universe, who has
created all things to Your glory.

Blessed are You, Adonai our God, Source of the universe, Creator
of humankind.

Blessed are You, Adonai our God, Source of the universe, who has
made man in Your image after Your likeness, and has fashioned
woman from man as his companion, that together they may perpet-
uate life. Blessed are You, Adonai, Creator of humankind.

May Zion rejoice as her children are restored to her in joy. Blessed
art You, Adonai, who causes Zion to rejoice at her children's return.

Make this bride and groom into loving companions, just as You did
the creatures in the Garden of Eden. Blessed art You, Adonai, who
bestows lasting joy on groom and bride.

In addition to the seven traditional blessings, some
Jewish couples choose to
add an eighth blessing in
recognition that gay and
lesbian couples are granted
the same religious, legal,
and social privileges as het-
erosexual couples. Biblical
passages may be read that
express the devotion be-
tween Ruth and Naomi and
the adoration between
Jonathan and King David.
The bride and groom may
also spill out a few drops
from their wineglass to
demonstrate that they cannot fully rejoice until all loving relationships are
accepted equally.

Blessed are You, Adonai our God, Source of the universe, who has created joy and gladness, bride and groom, mirth and exultation, pleasure and delight, love and friendship, peace and fellowship. May we all see the day when the sounds of joy fill the streets of Jerusalem and echo throughout the world, as the voices of the groom and the bride, the jubilant voices of those joined in marriage under the bridal canopy, and of youths feasting and singing. Blessed are You, Adonai, who rejoices with the bride and groom.

Buddhist Marriage Homily

Nothing happens without a cause. The union of this man and woman has not come about accidentally but is the foreordained result of many past lives. This tie can therefore not be broken or resolved.

In the future, happy occasions will come as surely as the morning. Difficult times will come as surely as night. When things go joyously, meditate according to the Buddhist tradition. When things go badly, meditate. Meditation in the manner of the Compassionate Buddha will guide your life.

To say the words *love* and *compassion* is easy. But to accept that love and compassion are built upon patience and perseverance is not easy. Your marriage will be firm and lasting if you remember this.

Cultural Readings and Blessings

I know not whether thou has been absent:
I lie down with thee, I rise up with thee,
In my dreams thou art with me.
If my eardrops tremble in my ears,
I know it is thou moving within my heart.

—*Aztec love song*

Let the earth of my body be mixed with the earth
my beloved walks on.
Let the fire of my body be the brightness

in the mirror that reflects his face.
Let the water of my body join the waters
of the lotus pool he bathes in
Let the breath of my body be air
lapping his tired limbs.
Let me be sky, and moving through me
the cloud-dark Shyama, my beloved.

—*Hindu love poem*

O how big is my beloved
More than all the ones I know.
O how lively does my heart beat
When I only see him glow.
Love can never be forced;
Treat it fondly, it will grow.

—*Zanzibar*

Rising Sun! when you shall shine,
Make this house happy,
Beautify it with your beams;
Make this house happy,
God of Dawn! your white blessings spread;
Make this house happy.
Guard the doorway from all evil;
Make this house happy.
White corn! Abide herein;
Make this house happy.
Soft wealth! May this hut cover much;
Make this house happy.
Heavy Rain! Your virtues send;
Make this house happy.
Corn Pollen! Bestow content;
Make this house happy.
May peace around this family dwell;
Make this house happy.

—*Navajo chant*

You are my husband/wife.
My legs run because of you.
My feet dance because of you.
My heart shall beat because of you.
My eyes see because of you.

My mind thinks because of you.
And I shall love because of you.

— *Eskimo love song*

Now you will feel no rain,
for each of you will be shelter to the other.

Now you will feel no cold,
for each of you will be warmth to the other.

Now there is no loneliness for you;
now there is no more loneliness.

Now you are two bodies,
but there is only one life before you.

Go now to your dwelling place,
and enter into your days together.

And may your days be good
and long upon the earth.

— *Apache song*

In our next life,
We will be birds flying wing to wing in the sky,
Or sturdy branches entangled with each other on the earth.

— *Bai Ju-yi*
Tang Dynasty, China
Translation by Richard Liu

Fair is the white star of twilight, and the sky clearer at the
    day's end;
But she is fairer, and she is dearer,
She, my heart's friend.

Fair is the white star of twilight, and the moon roving to the
    sky's end;
But she is fairer, better worth loving,
She, my heart's friend.

— *Traditional Shoshone love poem*

God in heaven above please protect the ones we love.
We honor all you created as we pledge our hearts and lives together.
We honor mother earth—and ask for our marriage to be abundant
    and grow stronger through the seasons;
We honor fire—and ask that our union be warm and glowing with
    love in our hearts;

We honor wind—and ask we sail through life safe and calm as in
   our father's arms;
We honor water—to clean and soothe our relationship, that it may
   never thirst for love;
With all the forces of the universe you created, we pray for harmony
and true happiness as we forever grow young together.

   —*Cherokee prayer*

Poetry and Prose

The Couple's Tao Te Ching: "See Clearly"

Lau Tzu, sixth century B.C.E.
Interpreted by William Martin

   Your love is a great mystery.
   It is like an eternal lake
   whose waters are always still and clear like glass.
   Looking into it you can see
   the truth about your life.

   It is like a deep well
   whose waters are cool and pure.
   Drinking from it you can be reborn.

   You do not have to stir the waters
   or dig the well.
   Merely see yourself clearly
   And drink deeply.

The Couple's Tao Te Ching: "Always Return"

Lau Tzu, sixth century B.C.E.
Interpreted by William Martin

   It is good to know your strength
   but always return to your flexibility.
   If you can cradle your beloved in your arms
   in nurturing gentleness,
   love will flow through you.

   It is good to achieve things
   but always return to anonymity.
   Your beloved does not need your achievements
   but needs your uncomplicated soul.

. . .

It is good to work for change,
but always return to what is.
If you accept all things whether painful or joyful,
you will always know
that you belong to each other
and to the Tao.

The Couple's Tao Te Ching: "A Sacred Space"

Lau Tzu, sixth century B.C.E.
Interpreted by William Martin

Your love requires space in which to grow.
This space must be safe enough
to allow your hearts to be revealed.
It must offer refreshment for your spirits
and renewal for your minds.
It must be a space made sacred
by the quality of your honesty,
attention, love, and compassion.
It may be anywhere,
inside or out,
but it must exist.

The Couple's Tao Te Ching: "Transforming Power"

Lau Tzu, sixth century B.C.E.
Interpreted by William Martin

Your love contains the power
of a thousand suns.
It unfolds as naturally and effortlessly
as does a flower,
and graces the world with its blooming.
Its beauty radiates a transforming energy
that enlivens all who see it.
Because of you, compassion and joy
are added to the world.
That is why the stars sing together
because of your love.

"This Marriage"

Rumi, thirteenth century
Translated by Coleman Barks with A. J. Arberry

> This marriage be wine with halvah, honey dissolving in milk.
> This marriage be the leaves and fruit of a date tree.
> This marriage be women laughing together for days on end.
> This marriage, a sign for us to study.
> This marriage, beauty.
> This marriage, a moon in a light blue sky.
> This marriage, this silence fully mixed with spirit.

"In Love That Long"

Jelaluddin Rumi, thirteenth century
Translated by Coleman Barks

> I am here, this moment, inside the beauty,
> the gift God has given,
> Our love:
>   This gold and circular sign
> means we are free of any duty:
>   out of eternity
> I turn my face to you, and into
> eternity:
>   We have been in
> love that long.

"He Will Praise His Lady"

Guido Guinizelli, thirteenth century
Translated by Dante Gabriel Rossetti

> Yea, let me praise my lady whom I love:
> Likening her unto the lily and rose:
> Brighter than morning star her visage glows;
> She is beneath even as her Saint above;
>
> She is as the air in summer which God wove
> Of purple and of vermilion glorious;
> As gold and jewels richer than man knows.
> Love's self, being love for her, must holier prove.
> Ever as she walks she hath a sober grace,
>
> Making bold men abashed and good men glad;
> If she delight thee not, thy heart must err.
> No man dare look on her, his thoughts being base:

Nay, let me say even more than I have said; —
No man could think base thoughts who looked on her.

From *The Divine Comedy*

Dante Alighieri, thirteenth to fourteenth century

The love of God, unutterable and perfect, flows into a pure soul the way light rushes into a transparent object. The more love we receive, the more love we shine forth; so that, as we grow clear and open, the more complete the joy of loving is. And the more souls who resonate together, the greater the intensity of their love for, mirror-like, each soul reflects the other.

"Married Love"

Kuan Tao-shêng, thirteenth century
Translated by Kenneth Rexroth

You and I
Have so much love,
That it
Burns like a fire,
In which we bake a lump of clay
Molded into a figure of you
And a figure of me.
Then we take both of them,
And break them into pieces,
And mix the pieces with water,
And mold again a figure of you,
And a figure of me.
I am in your clay.
You are in my clay.
In life we share a single quilt.
In death we will share one coffin.

"My True Love Hath My Heart"

Sir Philip Sidney, sixteenth century

My true love hath my heart and I have his,
By just exchange, one for another given;
I hold his dear, and mine he cannot miss;
There never was a better bargain driven.
My heart in me keeps him and me in one;

My heart in him his thoughts and senses guides;
He loves my heart, for once it was his own;
I cherish his, because in me it bides.

My true love hath my heart and I have his.

"The Passionate Shepherd to His Love"

Christopher Marlowe, sixteenth century

Come live with me and be my love,
And we will all the pleasures prove
That hills and valleys, dales and fields
And all the craggy mountains yields.

There we will sit upon the rocks
And see the shepherds feed their flocks,
By shallow rivers to whose falls
Melodious birds sing madrigals.

And I will make thee beds of roses
With a thousand fragrant posies
A cap of flowers and a kirtle
Embroidered all with leaves of myrtle.

A gown made of the finest wool
Which from our pretty lambs we pull;
Fair lined slippers for the cold,
With buckles of the purest gold;

A belt of straw and ivy buds,
With coral clasps and amber studs:
And if these pleasure may thee move,
Come live with me and be my love.

The shepherds' swains shall dance and sing
For thy delight each May morning:
If these delights thy mind may move,
Then live with me and be my love.

"So Well I Love Thee"

Michael Drayton, sixteenth to seventeenth century

So well I love thee, as without thee I
Love nothing; if I might choose, I'd rather die
Than be one day debarr'd thy company.

. . .

Since beasts, and plants do grow, and live and move,
Beasts are those men, that such a life approve,
He only lives, that deadly is in love.

The corn that in the ground is sown first dies
And of one seed do many ears arise:
Love, this world's corn, by dying multiplies.

The seeds of love first by thy eyes were thrown
Into a ground untill'd, a heart unknown
To bear such fruit, till by thy hands 'twas sown.

Look as your looking-glass by chance may fall,
Divide and break in many pieces small
And yet shows forth the selfsame face in all:

Proportions, features, graces just the same,
And in the smallest piece as well the name
Of fairest one deserves, as in the richest frame.

So all my thoughts are pieces but of you
Which put together makes a glass so true
As I therein no other's face but yours can view.

Sonnet XVIII

William Shakespeare, sixteenth to seventeenth century

Shall I compare thee to a summer's day?
Thou art more lovely and more temperate:
Rought winds do shake the darling buds of May,
And summer's lease hath all too short a date:
Sometimes too hot the eye of heaven shines,
And often is his gold complexion dimm'd,
And every fair from fair sometime declines,
By chance, or nature's changing course, untrim'd,
But thy eternal summer shall not fade,
Nor loose possession of that fair thou ow'st,
Nor shall death brag thou wandr'st in his shade,
When in eternal lines to time thou gro'st,
  So long as men can breathe, or eyes can see,
  So long lives this, and this gives life to thee.

Sonnet CXVI

William Shakespeare, sixteenth to seventeenth century

Let me not to the marriage of true minds
Admit impediments. Love is not love
Which alters when it alteration finds,
Or bends with the remover to remove:
O, no! It is an ever-fixed mark,
That looks on tempests and is never shaken;
It is the star to every wandering bark,
Whose worth's unknown, although his height be taken.
Love's not Time's fool, though rosy lips and cheeks
Within his bending sickle's compass come;
Love alters not with his brief hours and weeks,
But bears it out even to the edge of doom.
    If this is error, and upon me prov'd,
    I never writ, nor no man ever lov'd.

Sonnet LXXV

William Shakespeare, sixteenth to seventeenth century

So are you to my thoughts as food to life,
Or as sweet-season'd showers are to the ground;
And for the peace of you I hold such strife
As 'twixt a miser and his wealth is found;
Now proud as an enjoyer, and anon
Doubting the filching age will steal his treasure;
Now counting to be with you alone,
Then better'd that the world may see my pleasure:
Sometimes all full with feasting on your sight,
And by and by clean starved for a look;
Possessing or pursuing no delight,
Save what is had or must from you be took.
    Thus do I pine and surfeit day by day,
    Or gluttoning on all, or all away.

"A Valediction: Forbidding Mourning"

John Donne, sixteenth to seventeenth century

As virtuous men pass mildly away,
And whisper to their souls to go,
Whilst some of their sad friends do say
The breath goes now, and some say no,

. . .

So let us melt, and make no noise,
No tear-floods, nor sigh-tempests move;
'Twere profanation of our joys
To tell the laity our love.

Moving of the earth brings harms and fears,
Men reckon what it did and meant;
But trepidation of the spheres
Though greater far, is innocent.

Dull sublunary lovers' love
(Whose soul is sense) cannot admit
Absence, because it doth remove
Those things which elemented it.

But we, by a love so much refined
That our selves know not what it is,
Inter-assured of the mind
Care less, eyes, lips and hands to miss.

Our two souls therefore, which are one,
Though I must go, endure not yet
A breach, but an expansion,
Like gold to airy thinness beat.

If they be two, they are two so
As stiff twin compasses are two:
Thy soul, the fixed foot, makes no show
To move, but doth, if the other do;

And though it in the center sit,
Yet when the other far doth roam
It leans, and hearkens after it,
And grows erect, as that comes home.

Such wilt thou be to me, who must,
Like the other foot, obliquely run;
Thy firmness makes my circle just,
And makes me end where I begun.

From *Paradise Lost*

John Milton, seventeenth century

That what seemed fair in all the world seemed now
Mean, or in her summed up, in her contained,

And in her looks, which from that time infused
Sweetness into my heart, unfelt before,
And into all things from her air inspired
The spirit of love and amorous delight.

When I approach
Her loveliness, so absolute she seems,
And in herself complete, so well to know
Her own, that what she wills to do or say
Seems wisest, virtuousest, discreetest, best;
All higher knowledge in her presence falls
Degraded, wisdom in discourse with her
Loses discountenance, and like folly shows.

"There Is No Happier Life but in a Wife"

William Cavendish, seventeenth century

There is no happier life
But in a wife,
The comforts are so sweet
When two do meet.
'Tis plenty, peace, a calm
Like dropping balm;
Love's weather is so fair,
Like perfumed air.
Each word such pleasure brings
Like soft-touched strings;
Love's passion moves the heart
On either part;
Such harmony together,
So pleased in either.
No discords; concords still,
Sealed with one will.
By love, God made man one,
Yet not alone.
Like stamps of king and queen
It may be seen.
Two figures on one coin,
So do they join,
Only they not embrace.
We, face to face.

"My Luve's Like a Red, Red Rose"

Robert Burns, eighteenth century

O, my luve's like a red, red rose
That's newly sprung in June;
O, my luve's like the melodie
That's sweetly played in tune.

As fair thou are, my bonnie lass,
So deep in luve am I;
And I will luve thee still, my dear,
Till a' the seas gang dry.

Till a' the seas gang dry, my dear,
And the rocks melt wi' the sun;
I will luve thee still, my dear,
While the sands o' life shall run.

Sonnet XIV

Elizabeth Barrett Browning
From *Sonnets from the Portuguese*, nineteenth century

If thou must love me, let it be for nought
Except for love's sake only. Do not say,
"I love her for her smile—her look—her way
Of speaking gently,—for a trick of thought
That falls in well with mine, and certes brought
A sense of pleasant ease on such a day."—
For these things in themselves, Beloved, may
Be changed, or change for thee,—and love, so wrought,
May be unwrought so. Neither love me for
Thine own dear pity's wiping my cheeks dry,—
A create might forget to weep, who bore
Thy comfort long, and lose thy love thereby!
But love me for love's sake, that evermore
Thou may best love on, through love's eternity.

Sonnet XLIII

Elizabeth Barrett Browning
From *Sonnets from the Portuguese*, nineteenth century

How do I love thee? Let me count the ways.
I love thee to the depth and breadth and height
My soul can reach, when feeling out of sight

For the ends of Being and ideal Grace.
I love thee to the level of everyday's
Most quiet need, by sun and candlelight.
I love thee freely, as men strive for Right;
I love thee purely, as they turn from Praise.
I love thee with the passion put to us
In my old griefs, and with my childhood's faith.
I love thee with a love I seems to lose
With my lost saints,—I love thee with the breath,
Smiles, tears, of all my life!—and, if God choose,
I shall but love thee better after death.

Sonnet XXII

Elizabeth Barrett Browning
From *Sonnets from the Portuguese*, nineteenth century

When our two souls stand up erect and strong,
Face to face, silent, drawing nigh and nigher,
Until the lengthening winds break into fire
At either curved point,—what bitter wrong
Can the earth do us, that we should not long
Be here contented! Think. In mounting higher,
The angels would press on us and aspire
To drop some golden orb of perfect song
Into our deep, dear silence. Let us stay
Rather on earth, Beloved,—where the unfit
Contrarious mood of men recoil away
And isolate pure spirits, and permit
A place to stand and love in for a day
With darkness and the death-hour rounding it.

Sonnet XII

Elizabeth Barrett Browning
From *Sonnets from the Portuguese*, nineteenth century

Indeed this very love which is my boast,
And which, when rising up from breast to brow,
Doth crown me with a ruby large enow
To draw men's eyes and prove the inner cost—
This love even, all my worth, to the uttermost,
I should not love withal, unless that thou
Hadst set me an example, shown me how,
When first thine earnest eyes with mine were crossed,

Readings

And love called love. And thus, I cannot speak
Of love even, as a good thing of my own:
Thy soul hath snatched up mine all faint and weak,
And places it by thee on a golden throne—
And that I love (O soul, we must be meek!)
Is by thee only whom I love alone.

Sonnet XXIV

Elizabeth Barrett Browning
From *Sonnets from the Portuguese*, nineteenth century

Let the world's sharpness like a clasping knife,
Shut in upon itself and do no harm
In this close hand of Love, now soft and warm,
And let us hear no sound of human strife
After the click of the shutting. Life to life —
I lean upon thee, Dear, without alarm
And feel as safe as guarded by a charm
Against the stab of worldlings, who if rife
Are weak to injure. Very whitely still
The lilies of our lives may reassure
Their blossoms from their roots, accessible
Alone to heavenly dues that drop not fewer,
Growing straight, out of man's reach, on the hill.
God only, who made us rich, can make us poor.

"The Newly-Wedded"

Winthrop MacKworth Praed, nineteenth century

Now the rite is duly done,
Now the word is spoken,
And the spell has made us one
Which may ne'er be broken;
Rest we, dearest, in our home,
Roam we o'er the heather:
We shall rest, and we shall roam,
Shall we not? together.

From this hour the summer rose
Sweeter breathes to charm us;
From this hour the winter snows
Lighter fall to harm us:
Fair or foul—on land or sea—

Come the wind or weather,
Best and worst whate'er they be,
We shall share together.

Death, who friend from friend can part,
Brother rend from brother,
Shall but link us, heart and heart,
Closer to each other:
We will call his anger play,
Deem his dart a feather,
When we meet him on our way
Hand in hand together.

"I Will Tell Thee What It Is to Love"

Charles Swain, nineteenth century

Love? I will tell thee what it is to love!
It is to build with human thoughts a shrine,
Where Hope sits brooding like a beauteous dove;
Where Time seems young, and Life a thing divine.
All tastes, all pleasures, all desires combine
To consecrate this sanctuary of bliss.
Above, the stars in cloudless beauty shine;
Around, the streams their flowery margins kiss;
And if there's heaven on earth, that heaven is surely this.

Yes, this love, the steadfast and the true,
The immortal glory which hath never set;
The best, the brightest boon the heart e'er knew;
Of all life's sweets the very sweetest yet!
O' who but can recall the eve they met
To breathe, in some green walk, their first young now?
While summer flowers with moonlight dews were wet,
And winds sighed soft around the mountain's brow,
And all was rapture then which is but memory now!

"Believe Me, If All These Endearing Young Charms"

Thomas Moore, nineteenth century

Believe me, if all these endearing young charms,
Which I gaze on so fondly to-day,
Were to change by to-morrow, and fleet in my arms,
Like fairy-gifts fading away,

Thou wouldst still be adored, as this moment thou art,
Let thy loveliness fade as it will,
And around the dear ruin each wish of my heart
Would entwine itself verdantly still.

It is not while beauty and youth are thine own,
And thy cheeks unprofaned by a tear,
That the fervor and faith of a soul may be known,
To which time will but make thee more dear!
No, the heart that has truly loved never forgets,
But as truly loves on to the close,
As the sunflower turns to her god when he sets
The same look which she turned when he rose!

"A Birthday"
Christina Rossetti, nineteenth century

My heart is like a singing bird
Whose nest is in a watered shoot;
My heart is like an apple-tree
Whose boughs are bent with thick-set fruit;
My heart is like a rainbow shell
That paddles in a halcyon sea,
My heart is gladder than all these,
Because my love is come to me.

Raise me a dais of silk and down;
Hang it with vair and purple dyes;
Carve it in doves and pomegranates,
And peacocks with a hundred eyes;
Work it in gold and silver grapes,
In leaves and silver fleur-de-lys;
Because the birthday of my life
Is come, my love is come to me.

"Love"
Christina Rossetti, nineteenth century

What is the beginning? Love.
What is the course. Love still.
What the goal. The goal is love.
On a happy hill.
Is there nothing then but love?

Search we sky or earth
There is nothing out of Love
Hath perpetual worth:
All things flag but only Love,
All things fail and flee;
There is nothing left but Love
Worthy you and me.

From *Wuthering Heights*

Emily Brontë, nineteenth century

. . . he's more myself than I am. Whatever our souls are made of, his and mine are the same. . . . If all else perished and he remained, I should still continue to be, and if all else remained, and he were annihilated, the universe would turn to a might stranger. . . . He's always, always in my mind; not as a pleasure to myself, but as my own being.

From *Jane Eyre*

Charlotte Brontë, nineteenth century

I have for the first time found what I can truly love—I have found you. You are my sympathy—my better self—my good angel—I am bound to you with a strong attachment. I think you

---

Readings to Make You Feel Young Again

Look to children's literature for sweet, fun readings to include in your ceremony. Here are a few places to start your search:

I Like You by Sandol Stoddard Warburg (Houghton Mifflin, 1990)

The Little Prince by Antoine De Saint-Exupéry (Harcourt Brace, 1968)

The Velveteen Rabbit by Margery Williams Bianco (Doubleday, 1958)

Corduroy by Don Freeman (Viking Press, 1985)

Made for Each Other by William Steig (HarperCollins Juvenile Books, 2000)

The Giving Tree by Shel Silverstein (HarperCollins Juvenile Books, 1986)

Guess How Much I Love You by Sam McBratney (Candlewick Press, 1995)

What the Dormouse Said: Lessons for Grown-ups from Children's Books, compiled by Amy Gash (Algonquin Books, 1999)

The Complete Poems of Winnie-the-Pooh by A. A. Milne (Dutton Books, 1998)

Readings

good, gifted, lovely: a fervent, a solemn passion is conceived in my heart; it leans to you, draws you to my centre and spring of life, wraps my existence about you—and, kindling in pure, powerful flame, fuses you and me in one.

"Love Is Enough"

William Morris, nineteenth century

Love is enough: though the World be a-waning,
And the woods have no voice but the voice of complaining,
Though the sky be too dark for dim eyes to discover
The gold-cups and daisies fair blooming thereunder,
Though the hills be held shadows, and the sea a dark wonder
And this day draw a veil over all deeds passed over,
Yet their hands shall not tremble, their feet shall not falter;
The void shall not weary, the fear shall not alter
These lips and these eyes of the loved and the lover.

"A Match"

Algernon Charles Swinburne, nineteenth century

If love were what the rose is,
And I were like the leaf,
Our lives would grow together
In sad or singing weather,
Blown fields or flowerful closes,
Green pleasure or grey grief;
If love were what the rose is,
And I were like the leaf.

If I were what the words are,
And love were like the tune,
With double sound and single
Delight our lips would mingle,
With kisses glad as birds are
That get sweet rain at noon;
If I were what the words are,
And love were like the tune.

If you were life my darling,
And I your love were death,
We'd shine and snow together
Ere March made sweet the weather

With daffodil and starling
And hours of fruitful breath;
If you were life, my darling,
And I your love were death.

If you were thrall to sorrow,
And I were page to joy,
We'd play for lives and seasons
With loving looks and treasons
And tears of night and morrow
And laughs of maid and boy;
If you were thrall to sorrow,
And I were page to joy.

If you were April's lady,
And I were lord in May,
We'd throw with leaves for hours
And draw for days with flowers,
Till day like night were shady
And night were bright like day;
If you were April's lady,
And I were lord in May.

If you were queen of pleasure,
And I were king of pain,
We'd hunt down love together,
Pluck out his flying-feather,
And teach his feet a measure,
And find his mouth a rein;
If you were queen of pleasure,
And I were king of pain.

From "Give All to Love"

Ralph Waldo Emerson, nineteenth century

Give all to love;
Obey thy heart;
Friends, kindred, days
Estate, good-fame,
Plans, credit and the Muse,
Nothing refuse.

'Tis a brave master;
Let it have scope:

Follow it utterly,
Hope beyond hope:
High and more high
It dives into noon,
With wing unspent,
Untold intent;
But it is a god,
Knows its own path
And the outlets of the sky.

It was never for the mean;
It requireth courage stout.
Souls above doubt,
Valour unbending.
It will reward,
They shall return
More than they were,
And ever ascending.

From "Song of the Open Road"

Walt Whitman, nineteenth century

Listen! I will be honest with you. I do not offer the old
smooth prizes, but I offer rough new prizes.

These are the days that must happen to you:
You shall not heap up what is called riches,
You shall scatter with lavish hand all that you earn or achieve.
However sweet the laid-up stores.
However convenient the dwelling,
You shall not remain there.
However sheltered the port, and however calm the waters,
You shall not anchor there.
However welcome the hospitality that welcomes you,
You are permitted to receive it but a little while.
Afoot and lighthearted, take to the open road,
Healthy, free, the world before you,
The long brown path before you leading wherever you choose.

Say only to one another:
Camerado, I give you my hand!
I give you my love more precious than money,
I give you myself before preaching or law:

Will you give me yourself? Will you come travel with me?
Shall we stick by each other as long as we live?

From *Letters to a Young Poet*

Rainer Maria Rilke, twentieth century
Translated by Stephen Mitchell

It is . . . good to love: because love is difficult. For one human
being to love another human being: that is perhaps the most difficult task that has been entrusted to us, the ultimate task, the
final test and proof, the work for which all other work is merely
preparation. . . . Loving does not at first mean merging, surren-
dering, and uniting with another person . . . it is a high induce-
ment for the individual to ripen, to become something in
himself, to become world, to become world in himself for the
sake of another person; it is a great, demanding claim on him,
something that chooses him and calls him to vast distances.

"There Is Nothing False in Thee"

Kenneth Patchen, twentieth century

There is nothing false in thee.
In thy heat the youngest body
Has warmth and light.
In thee the quills of the sun
Find adornment.

What does not die
Is with thee.

Thou art clothed in robes of music.
Thy voice awakens wings.

And still more with thee
Are the flowers of earth made bright.

Upon thy deeps the fiery sails
Of heaven glide.

Thou art the radiance and the joy.
Thy heart shall only fail
When all else has fallen.

What does not perish
Lives in thee.

From *The Little Prince*

Antoine de Saint-Exupéry, twentieth century
Translated by Katherine Woods

"One only understands the things that one tames," said the fox. . . . So the little prince tamed the fox . . . [*and the fox said*], "And now here is my secret, a very simple secret: It is only with the heart that one can see rightly; what is essential is invisible to the eye."

"What is essential is invisible to the eye," the little prince repeated, so that he would be sure to remember.

"It is the time you have wasted for your rose that makes your rose so important."

"It is the time I have wasted for my rose—" said the little prince, so that he would be sure to remember.

"Men have forgotten this truth," said the fox. "But you must not forget it. You become responsible, forever, for what you have tamed. You are responsible for your rose . . ."

"I am responsible for my rose," the little prince repeated, so that he would be sure to remember.

"The Old Song and Dance"

Kenneth Rexroth, twentieth century

You, because you love me, hold
Fast to me, caress me, be
Quiet and kind, comfort me
With stillness, say nothing at all.
You, because I love you, I
Am strong for you, I uphold
You. The water is alive
Around us. Living water
Runs in the cut earth between
Us. You, my bride, your voice speaks
Over the water to me.
Your hands, your solemn arms,
Cross the water and hold me.
Your body is beautiful.
It speaks across the water.
Bride, sweeter than honey, glad
Of heart, our hearts beat across
The bridge of our arms. Our speech
Is speech of the joy in the night

Of gladness. Our words live.
Our words are children dancing
Forth from us like stars on water.
My bride, my well beloved,
Sweeter than honey, than ripe fruit,
Solemn, grave, a flying bird,
Hold me. Be quiet and kind.
I love you. Be good to me.
I am strong for you. I uphold
You. The dawn of ten thousand
Dawns is afire in the sky.
The water flows in the earth.
The children laugh in the air.

"Tin Wedding Whistle"

Ogden Nash, twentieth century

Though you know it anyhow
Listen to me, darling, now,

Proving what I need not prove
How I know I love you, love.

Near and far, near and far,
I am happy where you are;

Likewise I have never learnt
How to be it where you aren't.

Far and wide, far and wide,
I can walk with you beside;

Furthermore, I tell you what,
I sit and sulk where you are not.

Visitors remark my frown
When you're upstairs and I am down,

Yes, and I'm afraid I pout
When I'm indoors and you are out;

But how contentedly I view
Any room containing you.

In fact I care not where you be,
Just as long as it's with me.

In all your absences I glimpse
Fire and flood and trolls and imps.

Is your train a minute slothful?
I goad the stationmaster wrothful.

When with friends to bridge you drive
I never know if you're alive,

And when you linger late in shops
I long to telephone the cops.

Yet how worth the waiting for,
To see you coming through the door.

Somehow, I can be complacent
Never but with you adjacent.

Near and far, near and far,
I am happy where you are;

Likewise, I have never learnt
How to be it where you aren't.

Then grudge me not my fond endeavor,
To hold you in my sight forever;

Let none, not even you, disparage
Such valid reason for a marriage.

From "Know Deeply, Know Thyself More Deeply"
D. H. Lawrence, twentieth century

Go deeper than love, for the soul has greater depths,
love is like the grass, but the heart is deep wild rock
molten, yet dense and permanent.

"Love Is"
Nikki Giovanni, twentieth century

Some people forget that love is
tucking you in and kissing you "Good night"
no matter how young or old you are

Some people don't remember that love is
listening and laughing and asking questions
no matter what your age

. . .

Few recognize that love is
commitment   responsibility   no fun at all
unless

Love is
You and me

"And I Have You"

Nikki Giovanni, twentieth century

Rain has drops   Sun has shine
Moon has beams   That make you mine

Rivers have banks   Sands for shores
Hearts have heartbeats   That make me yours

Needles have eyes   Though pins may prick
Elmer has glue   To make things stick

Winter has Spring   Stockings feet
Pepper has mint   To make it sweet

Teachers have lessons Soup du jour
Lawyers sue bad folks   Doctors cure

All and all this much is true
You have me   And I have you

From "Resignation"

Nikki Giovanni, twentieth century

I love you
because the Earth turns round the sun
because the North wind blows north
sometimes
because the Pope is Catholic
and most Rabbis Jewish
because winters flow into springs
and the air clears after a storm
because only my love for you
despite the charms of gravity
keeps me from falling off this Earth
into another dimension
I love you
because it is the natural order of things

"You Came, Too"

Nikki Giovanni, twentieth century

I came to the crowd seeking friends
I came to the crowd seeking love
I came to the crowd for understanding

I found you

I came to the crowd to weep
I came to the crowd to laugh

You dried my tears
You shared my happiness

I went from the crowd seeking you
I went from the crowd seeking me
I went from the crowd forever

You came, too

"somewhere i have never travelled,gladly beyond"

E. E. Cummings, twentieth century

somewhere i have never travelled,gladly beyond
any experience, your eyes have their silence:
in your most frail gesture are things which enclose me,
or which i cannot touch because they are too near

your slightest look easily will unclose me
though I have closed myself as fingers,
you open always petal by petal myself as Spring opens
(touching skilfully,mysteriously)her first rose

or if your wish be to close me,i and
my life will shut very beautifully,suddenly,
as when the heart of this flower imagines
the snow carefully everywhere descending;

nothing which we are to perceive in this world equals
the power of your intense fragility:whose texture
compels me with the colour of its countries,
rendering death and forever with each breathing

(i do not know what it is about you that closes
and opens;only something in me understands

the voice of your eyes is deeper than all roses)
nobody,not even the rain,has such small hands

Sonnet XVII

Pablo Neruda, twentieth century

I do not love you as if you were salt-rose, or topaz,
or the arrow of carnations the fire shoots off.
I love you as certain dark things are to be loved,
in secret, between the shadow and the soul.

I love you as the plant that never blooms
but carries in itself the light of hidden flowers;

Words of Wisdom

This reading was written by and meant to be recited by an officiant, but it would make a wonderful reading for a parent or a married sibling or friend to read.

Our wish for both of you today is that your marriage will bring much happiness and joy to each of you. Happiness in marriage is not something that just happens; a good marriage must be created. And it is created in the following ways:

It is never being too old to hold hands.

It is remembering to say "I love you" at least once a day.

It is at no time taking the other for granted.

It is having a mutual sense of values and common objectives.

It is standing together facing life.

It is forming a circle of love that gathers in the whole family.

It is doing things for each other not in the attitude of duty or sacrifice, but in the spirit of joy.

It is speaking words of appreciation and demonstrating gratitude.

It is not looking for perfection in each other.

It is cultivating flexibility, patience, understanding, and a sense of humor.

It is having the capacity to forgive and forget.

It is giving each other an atmosphere in which each can grow.

It is finding room for the things of the spirit.

It is a common search for the good and the beautiful.

It is establishing a relationship in which independence is equal, dependence is mutual, and obligation is reciprocal. It is not only marrying the right partner, it is being the right partner.

—BILL SWETMON, ordained nondenominational minister

Readings

thanks to your love a certain solid fragrance,
risen from the earth, lives darkly in my body.

I love you without knowing how, or when, or from where.
I love you straightforwardly, without complexities or pride;
so I love you because I know no other way

than this: where *I* does not exist, nor *you,*
so close that your hand on my chest is my hand,
so close that your eyes close as I fall asleep.

From *Marriage and Morals*

Bertrand Russell, twentieth century

The essence of a good marriage is respect for each other's personality combined with that deep intimacy, physical, mental, and spiritual, which makes a serious love between man and woman the most fructifying for all human experiences. Such love, like everything that is great and precious, demands its own morality, and frequently entails a sacrifice of the less to the greater; but such sacrifice must be voluntary, for, where it is not, it will destroy the very basis of the love for the sake of which it is made.

From *Love*

Leo Buscaglia, twentieth century

In discussing love, it would be well to consider the following premises:

One cannot give what he does not possess. To give love you must possess love.

One cannot teach what he does not understand. To teach love you must comprehend love.

One cannot know what he does not study. To study love you must live in love.

One cannot appreciate what he does not recognize. To recognize love you must be receptive to love.

One cannot have doubt about that which he wishes to trust. To trust love you must be convinced of love.

One cannot admit what he does not yield to. To yield to love you must be vulnerable to love.

One cannot live what he does not dedicate himself to. To dedicate yourself to love you must be forever growing in love.

From *The Prophet*

Kahlil Gibran, twentieth century

> Love one another, but make not a bond of love;
> Let it rather be a moving sea between the shores of your souls.
> Fill each other's cup but drink not from one cup.
> Give one another of your bread but eat not from the same loaf.
> Sing and dance together and be joyous, but let each one of you be alone,
> Even as the strings of a lute are alone though they quiver with the same music.
>
> Give your hearts, but not into each other's keeping.
> For only the hand of Life can contain your hearts.
> And stand together yet not too near together:
> For the pillars of the temple stand apart,
> And the oak tree and the cypress grow not in each other's shadow.

From *Corelli's Mandolin*

Louise De Bernières, twentieth century

And another thing. Love is a temporary madness, it erupts like volcanoes and then subsides. And when it subsides you have to make a decision. You have to work out whether your roots have so entwined together that it is inconceivable that you should ever part. Because this is what love is. Love is not breathlessness, it is not excitement, it is not the promulgation of promises of eternal passion. . . . That is just being "in love," which any fool can do. Love itself is what is left over when being in love has burned away, and this is both an art and a fortunate accident. Your mother and I had it, we had roots that grew towards each other underground, and when all the pretty blossom had fallen from our branches we found that we were one tree and not two.

"Two Trees"

Janet Miles, twentieth century

> A portion of your soul has been
>   entwined with mine.
> A gentle kind of togetherness, while
>   separately we stand.

As two trees deeply rooted in
    separate plots of ground,
While their topmost branches
    come together,
Forming a miracle of lace
    against the heavens.

"The Sonnet"

Arthur Davison Ficke, twentieth century

Love is the simplest of all earthly things.
It needs no grandeur of celestial trust
In more than what it is, no holy wings:
It stands with honest feet in honest dust.
And is the body's blossoming in clear air
Of trustfulness and joyance when alone
Two mortals pass beyond the hour's despair
And claim that Paradise which is their own.
Amid a universe of sweat and blood,
Beyond the glooms of all the nations' hate,
Lovers, forgetful of the poisoned mood
Of the loud world, in secret ere too late
A gentle sacrament may celebrate
Before their private altar of the good.

"Barter"

Sara Teasdale, twentieth century

Life has loveliness to sell,
All beautiful and splendid things,
Blue waves whitened on a cliff,
Soaring fire that sways and sings,
And children's faces looking up,
Holding wonder like a cup.
Life has loveliness to sell
Music like a curve of gold,
Scent of pine trees in the rain,
Eyes that love you, arms that hold,
And for your spirit's still delight,
Holy thoughts that star the night.
Spend all you have for loveliness,
Buy it and never count the cost;

For one white singing hour of peace
Count many a year of strife well lost,
And for a breath of ecstacy
Give all you have been, or could be.

"We become new"
Marge Piercy, twentieth century

How it feels to be touching
you : an Io moth, orange
and yellow as pollen,
wings through the night
miles to mate,
could crumble in the hand.

Yet our meaning together
is hardy as an onion
and layered.
Goes into the blood like garlic.
Sour as rose hips,
gritty as whole grain,

fragrant as thyme honey.
When I am turning slowly
in the woven hammocks of our talk,
when I am chocolate melting into you,
I taste everything new
in your mouth.

You are not my old friend.
How did I used to sit
and look at you? Now
though I seem to be standing still
I am flying flying flying
in the trees of your eyes.

"Unclench yourself"
Marge Piercy, twentieth century

Open, love, open.
I tell you we are able
I tell you we are able
now and then gently

Tomes of Love

These books may help spark more ideas for your readings.

Love in Verse: Classic Poems of the Heart, compiled by Kathleen Blease (Fawcett Books, 1998)

Love Letters (Everyman's Library Pocket Poets), edited by Peter Washington (Knopf, 1996)

Love Poems (Everyman's Library Pocket Poets), edited by Peter Washington (Knopf, 1993)

Love Songs and Sonnets (Everyman's Library Pocket Poets), edited by Peter Washington (Knopf, 1997)

A Book of Love Poetry, edited by Jon Stallworthy (Oxford University Press, 1986)

The World Treasury of Love Stories, edited by Lucy Rosenthal (Oxford University Press, 1995)

Into the Garden: A Wedding Anthology, edited by Robert Hass and Stephen Mitchell (HarperPerennial Library, 1994)

African-American Wedding Readings, edited by Tamara Nikuradse (Plume, 1999)

Passionate Love Letters: An Anthology of Desire by Michelle Lovric (Shooting Star Press, 1995)

Bartlett's Book of Love Quotations compiled by Barbara Ann Kipfer (Little Brown & Co., 1994)

Bartlett's Familiar Quotations compiled by John Bartlett. Edited by Justin Kaplan. (Little Brown & Co., 1992)

Word Lover's Book of Unfamiliar Quotations by Wesley D. Camp (Prentice Hall, 1999)

with hands and feel
cold even as fish
to curl into a tangle
and grow a single hide,
slowly to unknit all other skin
and rest in flesh
and rest in flesh entire.
Come all the way in, love,
it is a river
with a strong current
but its brown waters
will not drown you.
Let go.
Do not hold out
your head.
The current knows the bottom
better than your feet can.
You will find
that in this river
we can breathe
we can breathe
and under water see
small gardens and bright fish
too tender
too tender
for the air.

"Scaffolding"

Seamus Heaney, twentieth century

Masons, when they start upon a building,
Are careful to test out the scaffolding;

Make sure that planks won't slip at busy points,
Secure all ladders, tighten bolted joints.

And yet all this comes down when the job's done
Showing off walls of sure and solid stone.

So if, my dear, there sometimes seem to be
Old bridges breaking between you and me

Never fear. We may let the scaffolds fall
Confident that we have built our wall.

"The White Lilies"

Louise Glück, twentieth century

As a man and woman make
a garden between them like
a bed of stars, here
they linger in the summer evening
and the evening turns
cold with their terror: it
could all end, it is capable
of devastation. All, all
can be lost, through scented air
the narrow columns
uselessly rising, and beyond,
a churning sea of poppies—

Hush, beloved. It doesn't matter to me
how many summers I live to return:
this one summer we have entered eternity.
I felt your two hands
bury me to release its splendor.

"Both Together and Each Apart"

Yehuda Amichai, twentieth century

My girl, another summer's gone dark,
My father didn't come to the Luna Park.
The swings are swinging like our heart.
Both together and each apart.

The horizon loses the ship's prow—
It's hard to hold onto anything now.
Behind the mountain, the warriors are set.
We can use all the pity we can get.
Both together and each apart.

The moon is sawing the clouds above—
Come, let's start a duel of love.
Just the two of us will love before the hosts.
We may still change all evil ghosts.
Both together and each apart.

My love has made me, it is plain,
Like a salt sea in the first rain.

Slowly I am brought to you, I fall.
Take me. We have no angel at all.
Both together. And each apart.

"I Sat in the Happiness"

Yehuda Amichai, twentieth century

Your eyes withstood great cold
And great heat
Like beautiful glass
And remained clear.

I sat in the happiness. Like straps
Of a heavy knapsack,
Love cut the shoulders of my heart.

Your eyes forced on me
A history of new life.

I sat in the happiness. From now on
I will be just one side in the dictionary,
Expressed or explained.

Your eyes count and count.

For more ideas on readings or to submit your own selections,
visit www.theknot.com/readings

rings and other rituals

The wedding rituals of a culture or country, an ethnic or religious group, or even a family serve much the same purpose—they are tried-and-true symbols of the joining of two people in marriage. They are the ways the community—the people present at your wedding, but also everyone else who follows the same traditions and shares the same beliefs—recognizes the importance of the step the two of you are taking, and a way for you to take your places next to all the couples who came before you. They are also an ideal way to include the people close to you in your ceremony: Your mothers can light the candles for your unity candle ritual, or grandparents can take part in an African-American libation, for example. We've collected an array of the countless rituals you may choose to include—and, where applicable, the words that go with them.

Exchanging Rings

After you exchange vows, you will exchange wedding rings. Your officiant may say a few words first about their symbolism; if you're having a religious ceremony, your priest, minister, or rabbi will likely say a blessing over them, as well. Below are some phrases you can use during the exchange, or you may choose to compose your own. The most simple and traditional phrase: "With this ring, I thee wed."

Protestant/Presbyterian

In token and pledge of our constant faith and abiding love, with this ring I thee wed, in the name of the Father, and of the Son, and of the Holy Spirit. Amen.

Lutheran

I give you this ring as a sign of my love and faithfulness.

Receive this ring as a token of wedded love and faith.

Episcopal

I give you this ring as a symbol of my vow, and with all that I am, and all that I have, I honor you, in the name of the Father, and of the Son, and of the Holy Spirit [or: in the name of God].

Methodist

I give you this ring as a sign of my vow, and with all that I am, and all that I have, I honor you [in the name of the Father, and of the Son, and of the Holy Spirit].

In token and pledge of the vow between us made, with this ring I thee wed; in the name of the Father, and of the Son, and of the Holy Spirit. Amen.

Baptist

With this ring I thee wed, and all my worldly goods I thee endow. In sickness and in health, in poverty or in wealth, till death do us part.

Catholic

Take this ring as a sign of my love and fidelity. In the name of the Father, and of the Son, and of the Holy Spirit.

In the name of the Father, and of the Son, and of the Holy Spirit. Take and wear this ring as a pledge of my fidelity.

Unitarian

With this ring, I wed you and pledge you my love now and forever.

Jewish

Haray at mekudeshet lee beh-taba'at zo keh-dat Moshe veh-Yisrael: Behold, you are consecrated to me with this ring according to the laws of Moses and Israel.

Thou are consecrated unto me with this ring as my wife/husband, according to the laws of Moses and Israel.

Be sanctified to me with this ring, in accordance with the laws of Moses and Israel.

Nondenominational

With this ring, I thee wed, as a symbol of love that has neither beginning nor end.

I give you this ring; wear it with love and joy.

As this ring encircles your finger from this day forward, year in and year out, so will my love forever encircle you.

This ring I give you as a sign of our constant faith and abiding love.

I give you this ring as a reminder that I love you every day of your life.

This ring I give you in token of my devotion and love, and with my heart I pledge to you all that I am. With this ring I marry you and join my life to yours.

I offer you this ring as a symbol of my enduring love. I ask that you take it and wear it so that all may know you are touched by my love.

Go little ring to that same sweet
That hath my heart in her domain . . .

    —Geoffrey Chaucer

This ring is round and hath no end,
So is my love unto my friend.

    —Sixteenth-century vow

I give you this ring. Wear it with love and joy. As this ring has no end, neither shall my love for you. I choose you to be my wife/husband this day and every day.

    —Bill Swetmon, ordained nondenominational minister

With this ring, I give you my promise that from this day forward you shall never walk alone. My heart will be your shelter, my arms will be your home. We will walk together through life as partners and best friends. I promise that I shall always do my best to love and accept you exactly the way you are. With this ring, I give you your freedom and my trust in you. I give you my heart until the end of time; I have no greater gift to give.

> —*Joyce Gioia, multifaith clergywoman*
> *Adapted from* Illuminata: Thoughts, Prayers, Rites of Passage,
> *by Marianne Williamson*

More Exchanges

Almost all weddings, regardless of culture or religion, contain a ritual of exchange. The bride and groom may exchange flowers and food as a symbolic gesture, or they may exchange tangible objects, such as rings and money.

Triple Ring Exchange (Eastern Orthodox)

The wedding rings are blessed during the betrothal ceremony. After reciting blessings and biblical passages, the priest makes the sign of the cross while holding the rings and declaring the betrothal. He may hold the rings in his hands while pressing the foreheads of the couple three times each. Then, either the priest or the *koumbaros* (the best man) exchanges the rings between the couple's fingers three times, signifying that the weakness of one will be compensated by the other. Because the right hand has a rich and symbolic history in the Church, the rings are usually placed on the third finger of the right hand.

Crowning Ceremony (Eastern Orthodox)

The crowning is the centerpiece of an Eastern Orthodox wedding ceremony. Garland wreaths are often fashioned into ornate crowns as a symbol of glory and honor. Crowns can also be made of orange blossoms, myrtle leaves, or semiprecious stones and metals. Threads of gold and crimson are sometimes used to represent the royalty of marriage. The *koumbaros* presents the couple with two crowns joined by a white ribbon,

---

Words of Engravement

Here are some ideas for words of love engraved inside your wedding rings.

I love you

Our love is eternal

To my soul mate

T.G. to T.S. 10/06/2000

Always

Forever

∞ (eternity)

C & D forever (use your first initials)

I thee wed

All my love

I marry you

You have my heart

My heart is in your hands

Never to part

To my wife/husband

Soul mates forever

I'm always with you

To have and to hold

Schmoopie (Your private nicknames for each other)

Here is my heart, guard it well!

No one but you

God For Me Provided Thee

God Unite Both in Love

In Thy Brest My Hart

Doth Rest (Old English)

Por Tous Jours (For all days— 15th-century French)

continued →

symbolizing their union. The priest then places the crowns on the couple's heads while they face the altar. The *koumbaros* swaps the crowns on the couple's heads three times, symbolizing the Holy Trinity. According to ancient custom, the crowns are to stay with the couple for life—some couples are even buried in them.

Garland Exchange (Hindu and Hawaiian)

In both Hindu and Hawaiian ceremonies, the bride and groom exchange garlands of flowers. In Hindu weddings, the bride and groom meet in front of the *mandap* (wedding platform), where they exchange gifts of flower garlands before stepping onto the platform in a ceremony called *Kanya Baran Jaimala*. They then wear the garlands around their necks throughout the ceremony. Hawaiian couples exchange leis (the jewels of the ancient Hawaiians) and seal their union by rubbing noses.

Kola Nuts (Nigeria)

In Africa, kola nuts represent healing; giving them to each other (often after the vows) is a symbol of the couple's commitment to work out their differences and support each other through hard times.

Arras (Spanish and Latino)

During Catholic ceremonies in Spain, Panama, and Mexico, the groom presents the bride with thirteen gold coins, known as *arras,* to represent his ability to support her. The coins are blessed by the priest and passed through the hands of the newlyweds several times, ending with the bride. Want to make the ritual a little more balanced? Consider giving each other coins, to symbolize shared responsibility.

Meher (Muslim)

Included in the marriage contract is a *meher,* a formal statement specifying the monetary amount the groom will present to the bride. It is traditonally considered the bride's security and guarantee of freedom within the marriage. There are two parts to the *meher*: a "prompt," due before the marriage is consummated, and a deferred amount, given to the bride

Joie sans fin
(Joy without end—French)

Mon coeur est à vous
(You have my heart—French)

Je t'aime (I love you—French)

Mon amour
(My love—French)

En bien aimer
(To encircle with love—15th-century French)

Il mio cuore e il tuo per sempre
(My heart is yours forever—Italian)

Amore mio
(My love—Italian)

Myn Genyst
(My heart—Old German)

Mizpah
(God, watch between us when we are absent from one another—Hebrew, Genesis 31:48–49)

Ani L'dodi V'dodi Li
(I am my beloved's and my beloved is mine—Hebrew, Song of Solomon 2:16)

Semper amemus
(Let us always love—Latin)

Semper fidelis
(Always faithful—Latin)

Pari passu
(With equal step—Latin)

Amor vincit omnia
(Love conquers all—Latin)

Deus nos iunxit
(God joined us—Latin)

throughout her life. Today, many couples use the ring as the prompt, since the groom presents it during the ceremony; the deferred amount can be a small sum offered as a formality, or it can actually be a gift of money, land, jewelry, or even an education. The gift remains the bride's to use as she pleases.

Rose Ceremony (Nondenominational)

This modern ritual incorporates one of the most beloved symbols of romantic love—the rose. A white one is used in honor of the wedding day.

GROOM (*handing bride the rose*): _____, take this rose as a symbol of my love. It began as a tiny bud and blossomed, just as my love for you has grown and blossomed.

BRIDE (*placing rose into a bud vase filled with water*): I take this rose, a symbol of your love, and I place it into water, a symbol of life. For, just as this rose cannot survive without water, I cannot survive without you.

GROOM: In remembrance of this day, I will give you a white rose each year on our anniversary, as a reaffirmation of my love and the vows spoken here today.

BRIDE: And I will refill this vase with water each year, ready to receive your gift, in reaffirmation of my love and the vows spoken here today.

[At this time the couple may join hands around the vase to exchange their vows; or, this ritual can be done separately, after the vows have been spoken and rings have been exchanged.]

Giving Thanks

Wedding ceremonies are largely focused on the bride and groom, but their families are an important part of their marriage, and there are many rituals that recognize the couple's ancestors, their God, and the path that brought them to this day.

Libation Ceremony (Africa)

Libation is a traditional African ceremony in which water is poured on the ground in the four directions that the wind comes from in remembrance and honor of the couple's ancestors, calling on them to be present to witness the marriage. Often a family elder does the honors, and guests respond to the blessing with the word *ase,* meaning "so it may be." Here is a sample libation prayer:

> All praise to God Almighty. Praise to our African ancestors and roots. God gave his power for the roots of the trees to spread its branches wide. If man does not know his roots, then he does not know his God. Let the spirit of God and ancestors bring us closer in unity.

Homage to the Fire God, Agni (Hindu)

The following is recited over a ceremonial fire:

> "O Lord Fire, First Created Being! Be thou the over-lord and give food and drink to this household. O Lord Fire, who reigns in richness and vitality over all the worlds, come take your proper seat in this home! Accept the offering made here, protect the one who makes them, be our protector on this day, O you who see into the hearts of all created beings!"

Tea or Sake Ceremony (China and Japan)

It is part of the wedding ceremony for the couple to present their parents with tea (in China) or sake (in Japan), to show respect and to represent the new family bond. In a traditional Chinese tea ceremony, the bride serves tea with sugar to the groom and his family, the sweetness representing a wish for sweet relations. Japanese couples each drink three sips from three sake cups, then offer the rice drink to both sets of parents.

Unifying Rituals

There are many rituals that demonstrate the couple's commitment to each other and their new bond as a married couple. In many cultures, the hands of the bride and groom are literally tied together (giving us the popular phrase "tying the knot").

Handfasting (Afrocentric)

In some African tribes, the bride and groom have their wrists tied together with cloth or braided grass. To symbolize your own unity, have

DAWN AND DAVID

September 5

Oak Bluffs, Massachusetts

AT DAWN AND DAVID'S AFROCENTRIC WEDDING, the libation toaster held up the cup of water and said the following:

"An African proverb tells us that people who lack the knowledge of their past are like a tree without roots. So, in the spirit of remembrance, we pour this libation. We pour to honor the past, so that we may learn from it. We pour to honor the importance of family.

"We raise our cup to God to show our reverence for the original source of our lives. We use cool water to freshen the road our ancestors travel to be here with us today. We use cool water as a symbol of the continuity of life, to purify and to nourish our souls.

"We pour to celebrate the coming together of the families of David and Dawn. It is said that through others, we are somebody. Through this marriage, we broaden our family circle, remember our heritage, and recall those who gave us life.

"We call upon our ancestors—our mothers, grandmothers, and great-grandmothers, our fathers, grandfathers, and great-grandfathers, uncles, aunts, and cousins—the foundations of our families, immortalized in our thoughts.

"We call upon our elders, whose wisdom we seek in all endeavors. Our friends who we are blessed to have in our lives, our parents who guided us along the road to adulthood. We call upon family who have passed over and could not be here today. We ask that they be with us in our thoughts.

"We call upon the bride and groom, Dawn and David, that they may always find prosperity in love and devotion. We ask that this couple be blessed by children, because children give glory to a home.

"Therefore we cast our libations to the north, to the south, to the east, and to the west [toaster turned to the directions indicated as he spoke]. We wish everyone to leave more blessed than when they came. Amen."

Toasts adapted from *Jumping the Broom: The African-American Wedding Planner* by Harriette Cole (Henry Holt, 1995) and *The Nubian Wedding Book: Words and Rituals to Celebrate and Plan an African-American Wedding* by Ingrid Sturgis (Three Rivers Press, 1998)

your officiant or a close friend tie your wrists together with a piece of kente cloth or a strand of cowrie shells (symbols of fertility and prosperity) while affirming your oneness.

Handfasting (Celtic)

Handfasting was practiced by the Celts, among other people, during the Middle Ages. A year after the couple was handfasted they were officially considered a married couple. Many practicing pagans and Wiccans use the ritual as their wedding ceremony. It involves much reverence of nature and also the tying together of the bride's and groom's wrists or hands.

What follows are excerpts from a handfasting rite. There are many, many versions; go to books and Web sites to find the wording you prefer.

PRIESTESS: Welcome, friends, as we gather to celebrate the marriage of _____ and _____. Divine One, I ask thee to bless this couple, their love, and their marriage as long as they shall live in love together. May they each enjoy a healthy life filled with joy, love, stability, and fertility. (*turns to the east*)

Blessed be by the element of air. May you be blessed with communication, intellectual growth, and wisdom. (*turns to the south*)

Blessed be by the element of fire. May you be blessed with harmony, vitality, creativity, and passion. (*turns to the west*)

Blessed be by the element of water. May you be blessed with friendship, intuition, caring, understanding, and love. (*turns to the north*)

Blessed be by the element of earth. May you be blessed with tenderness, happiness, compassion, and sensuality. . . .

Love has its seasons, the same as does the Earth. In the spring of love is the discovery of each other, the pulse of the senses, the getting to know the mind and heart of the other; a blooming like the buds and flowers of springtime.

In the summer of love comes the strength, the commitment to each other, the most active part of life, perhaps including the giving of life back to itself through children; the sharing of joys and sorrows, the learning to be humans who are each complete and whole but who can merge each with the other, as the trees grow green and tall in the heat of the sun.

In the fall of love is the contentment of love that knows the other completely. Passion remains, and ease of companionship. The heart smoothes love into a steady light, glorious as the autumn leaves.

In the winter of love, there is parting, and sorrow. But love remains, as do the stark and bare tree trunks in the snow, ready for the renewal of love in the spring as life and love begin anew.

Now is the time of summer. _____ and _____ have gathered before their friends to make a statement of their commitment to each other, to their love.

(Couple faces each other) Do you now commit to each other to love, honor, respect each other, to communicate with each other, to look to your own emotional health so that you can relate in a healthy way, and provide a healthy home for children if you choose to have them; to be a support and comfort for your partner in times of sickness and health, as long as love shall last?

TOGETHER: We do.

[After the vows and ring exchange, the couple's hands are bound together in a "love knot." The priestess says something along the lines of: "With this cord, I bind you to the vows that you each have made."]

Handfasting (Egypt)

Marriages among the fellahin of Northern Egypt take place at night. The bride and groom, along with family and friends, walk through the streets to the church. As they walk, the men carry lanterns and the women sound the joyful *zagharit,* a shrill, vibrating call. When they arrive, the priest takes a silk cord and passes it over the groom's right shoulder and under his left arm, tying the thread into a looped knot. The priest says prayers and then unties the groom. He then ties the two wedding rings together with the cord. He questions the bride and groom on their intentions, then unties the rings and places them on the couple's fingers.

Hasthagranthi (Hindu)

The couple's hands are tied togther with string in a Hindu ritual called *Hasthagranthi.* This is followed by *Shakhohar,* the family roots union, in which the parents place their hands on top of the couple's to express their union as a family. A long scarf is then wrapped around the couple in a ritual called *Gath Bandhan.*

Circling the Table (Eastern Orthodox)

The priest (and sometimes the *koumbaros*, too) leads the couple three times around the altar on which a Bible and cross rest. This ritual predates Christianity—it originated in Judaism—and represents the dance around the Ark of the Covenant. The choir sings three hymns as the couple circles. In this act, they take their first steps as a married couple, with the Church (through the priest) leading them.

Circling (Jewish)

When the couple first step underneath the *huppah*, their wedding canopy, the bride circles the groom seven times, representing the seven wedding blessings and seven days of Creation, and demonstrating that the groom is the center of her world. To make the ancient ritual reciprocal, many couples opt to circle each other.

Lazo (Latino)

In Guatemala, the couple bind themselves together during the ceremony with a silver rope. Mexican couples perform a similar ritual, where a rosary or white rope is wound around their shoulders in a figure eight to symbolize their union. While the couple is bound together, the priest may recite the following: "Let the union of binding together this rosary of the Blessed Virgin Mary be an inspiration to you both. Remember the holiness necessary to preserve your new family can only be obtained by mutual sacrifice and love."

Symbolic Rituals

In some of the most ancient wedding rituals, the couple demonstrates their love and devotion by using symbolic objects, such as candles, food, and even brooms.

Seven Steps (Hindu)

After the couple has taken seven steps around the fire at their ceremony, their bond is sealed, and the following is recited in a ritual, *Saptha Padhi*. It also makes a beautiful reading on its own.

"We have taken the seven steps. You have become mine forever. Yes, we have become partners. I have become yours. Hereafter I cannot live without you. Do not live without me. Let us share the joys. We are word and meaning, united. You are thought and I am sound.

"May the nights be honey-sweet for us; may the mornings be honey-sweet for us; may the earth be honey-sweet for us; may the heavens be honey-sweet for us.

"May the plants be honey-sweet for us; may the sun be all honey for us; may the cows yield us honey-sweet milk!

"As the heavens are stable, as the earth is stable, as the mountains are stable, as the whole universe is stable, so may our union be permanently settled."

Honey Ceremony (Multifaith)

Multifaith clergywoman Joyce Gioia created this ritual revolving around honey, a symbolic food since ancient times and crossing many cultures.

"Honey is a symbol of the sweetness in life. And so, with this dish of honey, we proclaim this day as a day of great joy and celebration—a day to remember—Your Day. We thank you, Allah [or substitute deity name], for creating this divine substance, and ask you to bless it, even as you will bless this holy union. Amen."

[Groom dips his little finger into the honey and touches bride's tongue with it; bride does the same, touching groom's tongue.]

"As together you now share this honey, so may you, under God's guidance, in perfect love and devotion to each other, share your lives together, and thereby may you find life's joys doubly gladdening, its bitterness sweetened, and all things hallowed by time, companionship and love."

Unity Candle (Catholic)

This joining ritual is quite popular at Catholic weddings, but its significance is universal: the joining of the couple as a new family, as well as the merging of their two original families. Usually the officiant will explain the unity candle's meaning—the following is an example:

> "_____ and _____, the two separate candles symbolize your separate lives. I ask that each of you take one of the lit candles and that together you light the center candle.
>
> "The individual candles represent your lives before today. Lighting the center candle represents that your two lives are now joined to one light, and represents the joining together of your two lives and families to one."

After the candle is lit, your officiant or an honored friend or family member may recite a blessing, such as the following:

> "May the blessing of light
> Be with you always,
> Light without and light within.
> And may the sun shine
> Upon you and warm your heart
> Until it glows
> Like a great fire
> So that others may feel
> The warmth of your love
> For one another."

Candle Ceremony (Wiccan)

The words of this Wiccan candle ceremony focus on the couple's union in marriage. However, this candle ceremony focuses less on two families uniting (as a unity candle ceremony does) than on two indviduals coming together, yet remaining independent. Interfaith or nondenominational couples could certainly include it in their ceremony.

The priestess asks the bride and groom to each light a candle. Another candle stands unlit.

> "These two candles are yourselves. Each of you is a whole and complete human being. _____, speak to us of who you are. (_Groom describes himself._) _____, speak to us of who you are. (_Bride describes herself._)
>
> "Together, light the third candle, but extinguish not the first two. For in marriage you do not lose yourself; you add something new, a relationship, the capacity to merge into one another without

losing sight of your individual self. Together, speak to us of who you are as a couple." (*Bride and groom alternate speaking.*)

Candle Ceremony (Nondenominational)

Multifaith clergywoman Joyce Gioia is known for her personalized candle rituals. Here is an example, done with a central "eternal light" and two individual candles for bride and groom:

"Now, we're going to engage in a ceremony of spiritual symbolism. Ancient sages tell us that for each of us, there is a candle, a symbol of our own inner light, but that no one can kindle his or her own candle. Each of us needs someone else to kindle it for us. When two people fall in love, they kindle each other's candles, creating great light and joy and glorious expectations.

"_____ and _____, I'd like you to remember when it was in your relationship that you first realized you were truly in love and wanted to spend the rest of your lives together. And holding that thought . . .

"_____, take this candle (*groom picks up candle*), symbol of the inner light in _____. Light it by the eternal light, with the dedication to rekindle it again and again, whenever necessary. And _____, take this candle (*bride picks up candle*), symbol of the inner light in _____. Light it by the eternal light, with the dedication to rekindle it again and again, whenever necessary.

"With these candles, we can see how to achieve a beautiful marriage. In your marriage, you will try to bring these lights, the symbols of yourselves, closer and closer to each other, until they become one (*bride and groom join their flames and hold them together*)—one great torch of light, a radiant symbol of love, joy, peace, and harmony. This is the mystery of the union two becoming one.

"Yet, it is vitally important to remember that there are always really two (*bride and groom divide their flames*) in a marriage, each with his or her own desires, yearnings, dreams, and wishes. And these must be respected and responded to with great love, with great compassion, and with genuine tenderness.

"We know that it is the prayer of your beloved, as it is the prayer of each of us here, that you will continuously light these candles of love, so that there will always be light and joy, peace and harmony in your hearts and in your home (*bride and groom set candles down*).

"Please kiss each other."

Crossing Sticks (African-American)

Couples demonstrate their commitment by crossing tall wooden sticks in an African-American tradition that dates back to the time of slavery. The sticks represent the power and life force within trees. By crossing the sticks the couple expresses a wish for a strong and grounded beginning. If you decide to incorporate this tradition, you can choose large branches from both of your families' homes or a place meaningful to you as a couple.

Jumping the Broom (African-American)

An African tribal ritual had couples placing sticks on the ground to symbolize their home together. This may be the origin of broom jumping, which was popular among African-American slaves (who could not have official wedding ceremonies); it may also symbolize the sweeping away of evil spirits. The couple holds the broom together and sweeps in a circle while the officiant or a family elder talks about the significance of the ritual. Then the broom is placed on the floor and the couple joins hands. Everyone counts to three—then you jump!

Your officiant (or anyone really) can read this reworded version of a traditional slave marriage poem:

> "Dark and stormy may come the weather,
> This man and woman are joined together.
> Let none but him that makes the thunder,
> Put this man and woman asunder.
> I therefore announce you both the same,
> Be good, go long, and keep up your name.
> The broomstick's jumped, the world's not wide,
> She's now your own, go kiss your bride!"

Tasting the Four Elements (Yoruba)

In a ritual adapted from a Yoruba tradition, the bride and groom taste four flavors that represent different emotions within a relationship: sour

MELISSA AND STEVE

June 12

Wellesley, Massachusetts

FROM FOOD AND MUSIC to decorations and rituals, Melissa and Steve carefully planned their wedding weekend to reflect her Chinese heritage and his Jewish background. They set the tone for the big day with invitations that included a Chinese translation wrapped in handmade red paper, the Chinese color for good luck and fortune. They continued the red theme throughout their wedding day with overflowing urns of red flowers, red decorations, and red paper lanterns. Their ceremony, which they wrote themselves, was held beneath a quilted *huppah* made from squares of silk decorated by family and friends. After the ceremony, Melissa changed from her white wedding gown into a red Chinese *qi pao* with elaborate gold embroidery. She wore the *qi pao* during a Chinese tea ceremony, in which the couple served tea to their elders, who, in exchange, gave the newlyweds wedding gifts to wish them well. The Jewish-Chinese mix didn't stop there. The culinary delights of both cultures were combined in a wedding buffet that featured blintzes, potato pancakes, lo mein noodles, and fortune cookies. Even their band played a mix of klezmer and Chinese music.

(lemon), bitter (vinegar), hot (cayenne), and sweet (honey). By tasting each of the flavors, the couple symbolically demonstrates that they will be able to get through the hard times in life, and, in the end, enjoy the sweetness of their marriage.

Mala Badol (Bangladesh)

After the wedding feast, the ritual of *Mala Badol* is performed in Bangladesh and other South Asian countries. A thin cloth is placed over both the bride and the groom. They feed each other and share sips of *borhani* (a spicy yogurt drink) beneath the cloth. While looking at their reflection in a mirror, the bride and groom are asked, "What do you see?" They each answer with a romantic declaration, such as, "I see the rest of my life." The couple then exchange garlands of flowers. Recently, a new custom of exchanging rings has been added to the ritual.

Breaking the Glass (Jewish)

Crushing a wineglass under the groom's foot at the end of the ceremony is a Jewish tradition with many meanings. It's a symbol of the destruction of the First Temple in Jerusalem; a representation of the fragility of relationships; and a reminder that marriage changes the lives of individuals forever. Or, interpret it this way: Drinking the wine represents the joys and sweetness of life, and crushing the glass represents the hardships.

P'ye-Baek (Korea)

The bride offers dates and chestnuts—symbols of children—to the groom's parents while sitting at a low table covered with other symbolic offerings. The parents offer sake in return, and as a final gesture they throw the dates and chestnuts at the bride, who tries to catch them in her large wedding skirt. Although this ritual traditionally takes place a few days after the wedding, in the United States the *p'ye-baek* is often held right before the reception, with the bride and groom in full Korean costume. Family members may also offer gifts of money in white envelopes to the bride.

Gifts of Eggs (Muslim)

Eggs, which represent fertility and righteousness in Islam, are often given to the couple as symbolic gifts. The bride and groom may be handed eggs and showered with rice, candy, and dried fruit as they leave the reception.

Honey and Walnuts (Greece)

In some of the Greek islands, the wedding ceremony ends with honey and walnuts offered to the bride and groom from silver spoons. Walnuts are chosen because they break into four parts, symbolizing the bride, the groom, and their two families.

> **To research more rituals or to submit any of your favorites that we may have missed, visit www.theknot.com/rituals**

NOTES

programs and quotes

They're not mandatory, but wedding programs are wonderful keepsakes, and they will keep your guests in the loop as to who your attendants are, what readings and pieces of music will be performed, and what rituals will be included (especially if they are ethnic or religious customs with which not all of your guests are familiar). You can even tell the story of how you met and fell in love, share baby pictures, or honor your deceased grandparents in a program. Here's what to consider when creating yours.

Programming Notes

Your program can be as simple as a single printed sheet of paper (maybe in your wedding color), folded or flat, or as complex as a bound, printed booklet. Most are somewhere in between, often with several pages folded over and stapled, or held together by ribbon.

There are three ways to create your program. You can design it on a computer with a simple word-processing program, playing with different fonts; then simply print it out and make color or laser copies on nice paper, such as cotton, vellum, or parchment. If you (or a friend) are a graphic designer, you may use more complex software such as Quark Xpress or Pagemaker to create a sophisticated document with photos and typography that can then be professionally printed (or just xeroxed). Or, you can order your programs from an invitation catalog or your stationer; you may choose to have them done in the same colors and fonts as your invite. You supply the wording and the company or stationer creates the programs.

A basic program includes the following:

- On the cover (or at the top of the page if you do a single sheet), your names: "The marriage of Anna Sinclair and Robert Dixon"—and the wedding date.

FROM THE PRODUCERS

A Wedding Three Acts is another chapter in an already long story. It is the visible sign of what is already known to the two principals, that their love and friendship is something that doesn't come along very often, and is something they want to commit to for the rest of their lives. In order for you to fully get involved in this performance, it might be helpful for you to understand the events that led up to this day.

The Bride and Groom met in 1991, although they had been running in the same circles since 1988. Upon first meeting, the Bride did not like the Groom, and the Groom didn't even have an opinion about the Bride. A year later, they found themselves working together at a Leadership Camp sponsored by the Wisconsin Association of School Councils. They became casual acquaintances, always polite whenever their paths crossed, which was about once a year.

In 1997, they were selected to be two members of a nine member Board of Directors for the WASC TORCH BEARERS. The Board met six times a year – and for these meetings the Bride would fly to Madison to meet with her colleagues. Upon returning to New York, the Bride and Groom began a long-distance email dance that lasted for months. They fell in love in cyberspace – and they had never even been on a date.

Monthly visits became the norm, the Bride would fly to Minneapolis, the Groom would fly to New York, they met in Stevens Point to be staff members at another Leadership Camp, etc. The day after camp, the Groom proposed. One year ago.

Two months later, the Groom moved to New York City to be with his bride-to-be and to expand his career opportunities. The last year has been filled with much joy and laughter, and even with heartache. They've been thru so much in the last year. They've moved, started new jobs, gotten sick, gotten well, shared secrets, drank too much caffeine, went to the movies and the theatre, performed in bars, created websites, planned careers, worked on projects, quit their jobs, interviewed for new jobs, explored new cities...

... experienced daylight, and sunsets, and midnights, and cups of coffee, moved along in inches, in miles, shared laughter and pride... Throughout the last four seasons... their one constant was love. Many Seasons of Love... and many more to come.

The Producers

CAST

BRIDE	Sara Kuehl
GROOM	Derek Kosiorek
MAID OF HONOR	Mary Kuen
BEST MAN	Jeremy VanDinter
SARA'S FAMILY	Karen Kuehl, Mother of Bride
	Dr. Ronald C. Kuehl, Father of Bride
	Gail Zalewski, Stepmother of Bride
	Ryan Kuehl, Brother of Bride
DEREK'S FAMILY	Trudy Kemps, Mother of Groom
	Thomas Kosiorek, Father of Groom
	Donald Kemps, Stepfather of Groom
	Mary Jo Kosiorek, Stepmother of Groom
SARA'S SUPPORTING CAST	Anne Blaedow
	Cindy Bourquin
	Chris Heston
	Jess Jurkovic
	Damon Kinche
	Adam McCalvy
	Matt Miller
DEREK'S SUPPORTING CAST	David Anderson
	Ty Barwick
	Chad Brantmeier
	Woody Dean
	Dennis Downs
	Adam French
	Rusty Halverson
	Craig Kositzke
	Sean Svoboda
FLOWER GIRLS	Abby Kosiorek
	Megan Thiel
OFFICIANT	David Worzella

SARA AND DEREK

July 31

Stevens Point, Wisconsin

SARA AND DEREK'S WEDDING was definitely a production—complete with a *Playbill*! The theatrical couple's twenty-page program was designed to look exactly like those handed to Broadway theatergoers. Each guest at the theater in which the wedding took place was also handed a personalized ticket (complete with row and seat number). The elaborate booklet included "a producers note" explaining how Sara and Derek met; a "cast" list (from bride and groom to flower girls, with the attendants listed as "supporting cast"); an outline of the acts (Act One, the ceremony; Act Two, dinner; Act Three, dancing); and biographies and pictures of all the major players. Also included were excerpts from the e-mail the couple had exchanged while living 1,500 miles apart.

Sara created the program herself using Microsoft Publisher software; the cover was printed in color on shiny paper, and the inside was printed on regular copy paper. The wedding party helped put the programs together the day before the event. "Designing our program was my favorite part of the wedding," says the bride. "Our guests were able to better understand our relationship and the special people in our lives."

- The names of all the members of the wedding party, including friends and relatives who are reading or performing. You may also choose to include each bridesmaid's and groomsman's relationship to you ("college friend of the groom").
- The names of your parents and your officiant.
- The order of the ceremony so your guests can follow along. Include the names and writers/composers of the readings and songs used (you could also include the words of any poems that are read).

A more extended program may include:

- An explanation of any ethnic or religious rituals. Your officiant or a family member may be able to help you compose the words, or there may be a church or temple document you can borrow from. You don't need a four-page history, just enough to give people an idea of the ritual's overall significance.
- A heads up for any specific instructions for guests (e.g., most of a Quaker ceremony is silent, and guests are free to stand up at any time and say something to the couple).
- An "In Memoriam" for important family members who have passed away, or a special mention of those who are unable to attend. This can be done by writing a personal message or printing one of the honored person's favorite poems or songs. Many couples also thank their guests in the program.
- A recent photo of yourselves, pictures from your courtship, or favorite shots of the two of you as babies or children.

Programs should be handed out by ushers, by young assistants (a great role for those too-old-to-be-flower-girl types), or simply left on each seat (assign an attendant to the task).

For more information on programs or to submit
your ideas, visit www.theknot.com/programs

Programs
and Quotes

A Program Template

Here's a sample program to get you started working on yours. It's for a straightforward, fold-over program that's made like a book, with one "spread" inside. Or, you could also do it as a single flat page.

Cover:

The Wedding of

Katherine Emily Spade

and

Bradley Steven Bartlett

October 6, 2001

Chicago, Illinois

*Nothing is worth
more than this day.*

—Goethe

Inside page, left:

Our Wedding Party

Maid of Honor
Audra Spade, sister of the bride

Best Man
Kevin Bartlett, brother of the groom

Bridesmaids
Kristin Meyer, cousin of the bride
Taylor Baldwin, friend of the bride
Kelly Scott, friend of the bride

Groomsmen and Groomswomen
David Bartlett, brother of the groom
Marcus Daly, friend of the groom
Karen Carson, friend of the groom

Flower Girl
Carrie McDonnell, niece of the bride

Parents of the Bride
Kara and Colin Spade

Parents of the Groom
Sandra Kincaid
Steven and Maria Bartlett

Officiant
Rev. Thomas Stevenson

Readers
Michael Bartlett, cousin of the groom
Gina Dawson, friend of the couple

Our Ceremony

Prelude
"Longer," Dan Fogelberg
"My Romance," Rosemary Clooney
"Just in Time," Frank Sinatra

Processional
"Canon in D," Pachelbel

Welcome

Reading
From *The Prophet* by Kahlil Gibran

Interlude
"At Last"
Sung by the groom

Exchange of Vows and Rings

Reading
"Give All to Love" by Ralph Waldo Emerson

*At this time, Kate and Brad will light their unity
candle from candles lit by their mothers, Kara and
Sandy. This represents the joining of our two
families and the creation of our new family.*

Recessional
"All You Need Is Love," The Beatles

Reception begins at 6:30
at Oakwood Country Club. See you there!

*We'd like to thank
all our family and friends who
are here today—and we remember
those who can't be.*

*We love you all, and it means
so much to us to have you
share in our wedding day.*

—Kate & Brad

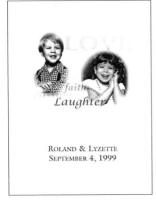

ROLAND & LYZETTE
SEPTEMBER 4, 1999

CEREMONY.
Queen of Angels Church, Chicago
Three o'clock in the afternoon.

Prelude
Selections featuring Beethoven & Bach.

LIGHTING OF CANDLES BY MOTHERS
OF THE BRIDE AND GROOM

Processional

ENTRANCE OF BRIDESMAIDS,
FLOWER GIRL, & MATRON OF HONOR
"Bist du bei Mir, (Art Thou With Me?)," J. S. Bach.

ENTRANCE OF BRIDE AND HER FATHER
"Trumpet Voluntary," Clarke.

Ceremony

OPENING PRAYER

A READING FROM THE OLD TESTAMENT:
Song of Songs 2:8–10, 14, 16a; 8:6–7a
Read By Alison McDonald

RESPONSORIAL PSALM, "ALL THE ENDS OF THE EARTH"

A READING FROM THE NEW TESTAMENT:
1 Corinthians 12:31–13:8a
Read By Walter Paulus

A READING FROM THE GOSPEL
ACCORDING TO JOHN 17:20–23

Rite of Marriage

EXCHANGE OF VOWS
BLESSING OF THE RINGS

Prayers & Blessings

PRAYER OF THE FAITHFUL
NUPTIAL BLESSING

Concluding Rite

THE LORD'S PRAYER

LIGHTING OF UNITY CANDLE
BY BRIDE AND GROOM

PRESENTATION TO THE BLESSED VIRGIN MARY
BY THE BRIDE

1 LASSO PRESENTED TO THE COUPLE

FINAL BLESSING

PRESENTATION OF THE COUPLE

Recessional
"Ode to Joy," Beethoven.

*Guests are asked to remain seated until the
wedding party reaches the back of the church.*

The Knot Guide
to Wedding Vows
and Traditions

LYZETTE AND ROLAND

September 4

Chicago, Illinois

PERSONALIZATION WAS A PRIORITY for Lyzette and Roland, who had pictures of themselves as children printed on the cover of their program (the same shots and words—*love, faith, passion, laughter*—graced their invitations). Inside, the program began with the story of how the couple met: "It gave people something to do while waiting for the ceremony to begin," says the bride. "Plus, we wouldn't have to explain how we met to those who didn't already know the story!" The next page listed the wedding party—the couple's parents, eight attendants, a flower girl, four ushers, and sponsors. (Lyzette's heritage is Mexican, and Hispanic couples often choose a "sponsor" couple, usually about their parents' age; Lyzette and Roland's sponsors participated by draping a beaded lasso around the couple's shoulders as a joining ritual during the ceremony.)

The order of the Catholic ceremony, including names of songs and readings, came next; Bach and Beethoven were featured composers, in honor of the groom's German background. Lyzette also had the reception menu printed in the program to whet guests' appetites, and on the last page thanked everyone who had made the wedding possible, from parents and attendants to her contact at the School of the Arts Institute, where the party was held.

Favorite and Famous Quotes

Include a meaningful quote about love, life, or friendship on the cover of your program—or even incorporate one into your invitation—to symbolize your relationship. You may already know the words that exactly express who you two are together. If not, here are some ideas; many can also be used in toasts. Also look to the readings on pages 32–75 for lines to excerpt.

Knowledge of what is possible is the
beginning of happiness.
　　—George Santayana

Who can doubt that we exist only
to love? Disguise it, in fact, as we will,
we love without intermission. . . . We
live not a moment exempt from its
influence.
　　—Blaise Pascal

Love is an act of endless forgiveness, a
tender look which becomes a habit.
　　—Peter Ustinov

What do I get from loving you? Loving
you.
　　—John-Roger

The goal of life should not be to find joy
in marriage, but to bring more love and
truth into the world. We marry to assist
each other in this task.
　　—Leo Tolstoy

To love someone is to see a miracle
invisible to others.
　　—François Mauriac

That Love is all these, is all we know of
Love.
　　—Emily Dickinson

Your embraces alone give life to
my heart.
　　—Ancient Egyptian saying

In our life there is a single color,
as on an artist's palette, which provides
the meaning of life and art. It is the
color of love.

—*Marc Chagall*

Thrice joyous are those united by an
unbroken bond of love, unsundered by
any division before life's final day.

—*Horace*

We are ordinarily so indifferent to people
that when we have invested one of them
with the possibility of giving us joy, or
suffering, it seems as if he must belong to
some other universe, he is imbued with
poetry.

—*Marcel Proust,* Remembrance of Things Past

However rare true love is, true friendship
is even rarer.

—*François, duc de La Rochefoucauld*

Those alone are wise who know
how to love.

—*Seneca*

The supreme happiness of life is the
conviction that we are loved.

—*Victor Hugo*

Love, love, love—that is the soul
of genius.

—*Wolfgang Amadeus Mozart*

To love is to place our happiness in the
happiness of another.

—*Gottfried Wilhelm Leibnitz*

We love because it's the only true
adventure.

—*Nikki Giovanni*

Two souls with but a single thought,
Two hearts that beat as one.

—*Fredrich Halm*

Love is all we have, the only way that
each can help the other.
　　—*Euripides*

It is the true season of love when we
know that we alone can love; that no one
could ever have loved before us and that
no one will ever love in the same way
after us.
　　—*Johann Wolfgang von Goethe*

When one has once fully entered the
realm of love, the world—no matter how
imperfect—becomes rich and beautiful,
it consists solely of opportunities for love.
　　—*Søren Kierkegaard*

Love will find a way.
　　—*Anonymous*

The greatest pleasure of life is love.
　　—*William Temple*

The greatest thing about love is that when
it's there, you know it.
　　—*Bill Cosby*

Marriage is serious business and hard
work. It's not just becoming roommates,
it's becoming soul mates; it's not just
signing a license, it's sharing a life. That
explains our title. The words in the
marriage ceremony "from this day
forward" *are* scary. At the moment a
couple exchanges those vows, they can
never know what they really mean, what
hills and valleys stretch out in front of
them in the years ahead. But if you take
the words seriously, there's no going back.
There's only the future, unlimited and
unknowable, and the promise to make the
journey together.
　　—*Steve and Cokie Roberts,*
　　　From the Introduction to
　　　From This Day Forward

Love is the joy of the good, the wonder
of the wise, the amazment of the Gods.
　　—*Plato*

Love is friendship set on fire.
　　—*Jeremy Taylor*

Love is a taste of paradise.
　　—*Sholom Aleichem*

Love is like pi—natural, irrational, and
very important.
　　—*Lisa Hoffman*

Marriage is the fusion of two hearts—the
union of two lives—the coming together
of two tributaries.
　　—*Peter Marshall*

Life is the flower of which love is the honey.
　　—*Victor Hugo*

Love doesn't make the world go 'round.
Love is what makes the ride worthwhile.
　　—*Franklin P. Jones*

Love is blind, but marriage restores its sight.
　　—*Georg Christoph Lichtenberg*

I have found the paradox that if I love
until it hurts, then there is no hurt, but
only more love.
　　—*Mother Teresa*

When love reigns, the impossible may be
attained.
　　—*Indian proverb*

Love is the greatest refreshment in life.
　　—*Pablo Picasso*

God created us so that we should form the human
family, existing together because we were made
for one another. We are not made for an exclusive
self-sufficiency but for interdependence, and we
break the law of being at our peril.
　　—*Desmond Tutu*

Who travels for love finds a thousand
miles not longer than one.
  —*Japanese proverb*

There is a single magic, a single power, a
single salvation, and a single happiness,
and that is called loving.
  —*Hermann Hesse*

A life without love is like a year without
summer.
  —*Swedish proverb*

Love is the only gold.
  —*Alfred, Lord Tennyson*

The best and most beautiful things in the
world cannot be seen or even touched.
They must be felt with the heart.
  —*Helen Keller*

If you would marry wisely, marry your equal.
  —*Ovid*

At the touch of love everyone becomes a
poet.
  —*Plato*

Harmony is pure love, for love is a
concerto.
  —*Lope de Vega*

Love is something eternal; the aspect may
change, but not the essence.
  —*Vincent van Gogh*

The only true gift is a portion of yourself.
  —*Ralph Waldo Emerson*

Mutual love, the crown of bliss.
  —*John Milton*

Never above you. Never below you.
Always beside you.
  —*Walter Winchell*

To love is to admire with the heart.
  —*Théophile Gautier*

When the one man loves the one woman
and the one woman loves the one man,
the very angels desert heaven and sit in
that house and sing for joy.
 —Braham Sutra

What's mine is yours and what is yours is mine.
 —*William Shakespeare,* Measure for Measure, *Act V*

Love demands all, and has a right to it.
 —*Ludwig van Beethoven*

I don't want to live. I want to love first,
and live incidentally.
 —*Zelda Fitzgerald*

Love is the master key that opens the gates
of happiness.
 —*Oliver Wendell Holmes*

Friendship is the marriage of the soul.
 —*Voltaire*

Marriage is the will of two to create the one
who is more than those who created it.
 —*Friedrich Nietzsche*

This is love—to fly upward toward the
endless heavens.
 —*Rumi*

Love is, above all, the gift of oneself.
 —*Jean Anouilh*

There is no remedy for love than to love
more.
 —*Henry David Thoreau*

Chief of all love's joys is in knowing we
love each other.
 —*George Eliot*

Love is you, you and me.
 —*John Lennon*

To love and be loved is to feel the sun
from both sides.
 —*David Viscott*

When two people are at one in their inmost hearts, they shatter even the strength of iron or of bronze.

—*I Ching*

The meaning of marriage begins in the giving of words. We cannot join ourselves to one another without giving our word. And this must be an unconditional giving, for in joining ourselves to one another we join ourselves to the unknown. . . . You do not know the road; you have committed your life to a way.

—*Ralph Waldo Emerson*

Love is supreme and unconditional; like is nice but limited.

—*Duke Ellington*

Marriage is like a golden ring in a chain, whose beginning is a glance and whose ending is eternity.

—*Kahlil Gibran*

Love keeps the cold out better than a cloak.

—*Henry Wadsworth Longfellow*

The only transformer and alchemist that turns everything into gold is love. The only magic against death, aging, ordinary life, is love.

—*Anaïs Nin,* The Diary of Anaïs Nin

Happy are they who enjoy an uninterrupted union, and whose love, unbroken by complaints, shall not dissolve until the last day.

—*Horace*

Love indeed is light from heaven, a spark of that immortal fire.

—*Lord Byron*

Deeper than speech our love,
Stronger than life our tether.

—*Rudyard Kipling*

There is nothing nobler or more admirable than when two people who see eye to eye keep house as man and wife, confounding their enemies and delighting their friends.

—*Homer,* The Odyssey

For more quotations or to submit your favorite, visit www.theknot.com/quotes

NOTES

music and dances

M ake no mistake: Well-selected wedding music is a must-have. In every culture, music is an important part of ritual—an inherent, practically crucial factor because of its ability to evoke emotion and bring people together. From the moment you walk down the aisle to the last dance at your reception, the songs you choose will color the day to make it uniquely yours (of course you'll want a band or DJ you can depend on, but be sure you have major input on the music that's played).

The Ceremony

The music you choose guides your guests through the ceremony, pumps up the emotion of what's taking place, and expresses your perspective, whether it's religious, cultural, or personal. Select songs that have meaning for you, that give you goosebumps, or that simply make you groove—whether they're traditional walking-the-aisle tunes, sultry standards, or evocative ethnic vibrations. Here's how:

- Before you do anything else, consider how *much* music you want played. Depending on how long and/or complex your ceremony will be, you may want several selections for the prelude (before the wedding begins), a processional and recessional, plus one or two additional selections during the ceremony itself—or you may just need a few snippets of music for when you walk in and walk out.

- Talk to your officiant. If you're having a religious ceremony, there may be guidelines and/or restrictions on the music you can play (for example, you may not be able to play secular tunes in some sanctuaries). If anything, the officiant and/or church organist can offer you ideas—a starting point for choosing appropriate music.

- If it's possible for you to include secular music in your ceremony, consider whether you'll stick with classical music—traditional or not—or other types of tunes for walking the aisle. Run your ideas by your officiant, if necessary.

* Next, figure out just where your ceremony music will be coming from—a church organist or pianist, perhaps with vocal accompaniment? a string quartet? a folk guitarist? a bagpiper? a CD? Members of the band you hire for your reception may be able to double as ceremony musicians, or your DJ may be able to play your selections if your ceremony will be held in the same place as your reception. Choose based on site restrictions (your church may dictate that their musical staff plays weddings) or the type of music you think you'd like.

Ceremony Musicians: Questions to Ask

Q: What are some good questions I can ask potential ceremony musicians?

A: When you talk to potential ceremony musicians, ask:

* Has he/she/the group done many weddings?

* Can you hear the musician play—either live or on a tape?

* What type of music does the musician specialize in? Does this jibe with what you envision? Does the musician have sheet music, or is he/she willing to purchase music for a song you'd like?

* How does the musician handle the stopping and starting of songs during a wedding so that they sound natural, not cut off unexpectedly? (Does it fade out seamlessly? Does the musician know precisely how long a version to play?)

* Will the musician bring his/her own equipment? Will anything else be needed (microphones, etc.)?

* If the musician will accompany in-house musicians at your site, is he/she available for a rehearsal?

* How much setup time will be needed?

* What is the musician's fee? Does he/she work by the hour?

Be sure to get written contracts from your ceremony musician(s), just as you would with any other wedding vendor, and consider whether you'll need the musician(s) present at your ceremony rehearsal. If you're having a long service with numerous musical selections, your officiant may want to talk to the musician(s) about cues, when to start/stop various pieces, etc.

Great Ceremony Selections

When you think about wedding music, you probably think "Here Comes the Bride." It's probably the most famous processional song, and there are others that are commonly used by thousands of marrying couples every year. The following lists are suggestions for your ceremony music from the prelude to the recessional, including traditional selections and some not-so-traditional tunes that we think would be wonderful for the right wedding—maybe yours.

The Prelude

Traditional / Classical

"Ave Verum Corpus in D major," Wolfgang Amadeus Mozart

"Brandenberg Concerto no. 4," Johann Sebastian Bach

"Brandenberg Concerto no. 3," Johann Sebastian Bach

"Clair de Lune," Claude Debussy

"Concerto for Harpsichord in F-minor, 2nd movement, Largo - Arioso," Johann Sebastian Bach

"Courante" from *Three Lute Dances,* Ludwig van Beethoven

"Grace," Georg Telemann

"Largo," *New World Symphony,* Antonin Dvořák

"O Mio Babbino Caro," Giacomo Puccini

Prelude to *Afternoon of a Faun,* Claude Debussy

"Prelude and Fugue in A," Johann Sebastian Bach

"Suite no. 3 for Orchestra," Johann Sebastian Bach

"Sonata for Piano no. 4 in E-flat major (1st movement, adagio)," Wolfgang Amadeus Mozart

"Symphony for Organ no. 5 in F-minor, op. 42, no. 1: 5th movement, Toccata," Charles-Marie Widor

"Trio for two flutes and harp from *L'Enfance du Christ,*" Hector Berlioz

"Variations in B-flat major on a theme by Haydn: St. Anthony Chorale," Johannes Brahms

"Waltz in A-Flat," Johannes Brahms

"Water Music Suite no. 1 in F: Air," George Handel

"Water Music Suite no. 1 in F: Menuet," George Handel

"Wedding Cantata," Johann Sebastian Bach

"Well-Tempered Clavier, Book 1: Prelude and Fugue no. 1 in C," Johann Sebastian Bach

Prelude Playlist

If you want music playing as guests are arriving and being seated, you will need to choose several selections (probably of a similar mood) totaling anywhere from ten to twenty minutes. Make a list of first choices (with times), but include a couple of extras on the list in case the bride gets caught in traffic or needs a final hair fix.

"At Last," Etta James

"Blue Skies," Ella Fitzgerald

"Chapel of Love," The Dixie Cups

"I've Got a Crush on You," Linda Ronstadt or
    Sarah Vaughan

"Just in Time," Frank Sinatra

"Let's Do It (Let's Fall in Love)," Louis Armstrong

"Longer," Dan Fogelberg

"Love Theme" from *Romeo and Juliet,* Henry Mancini

"My Funny Valentine," Eartha Kitt or Linda Ronstadt

"My Romance," Tony Bennett or Rosemary Clooney

"Rhapsody in Blue," George Gershwin

"Watch What Happens," Frank Sinatra or Tony Bennett

"Wedding Song," Bob Dylan

"What a Wonderful World," Louis Armstrong

"You'd Be So Nice to Come Home To," Ella Fitzgerald or
    Frank Sinatra

"You Make Me Feel So Young," Frank Sinatra

The Processional

Traditional/Classical

"Allemande," *G-Major Suite,* Johann Pachelbel

"Arioso," Johann Sebastian Bach

"Bridal Chorus" from *Lohengrin,* Richard Wagner

"Canon in D" for three violins and bass, Johann Pachelbel

"Carillon," Herbert Murril

"Crown Imperial," Sir William Turner Walton

"Fanfare for the Common Man," Aaron Copland

"Fantasia in G," Johann Sebastian Bach

"Jesu, Joy of Man's Desiring," Johann Sebastian Bach

"Majesty," Georg Telemann

"March" from *Scipio,* George Handel

"Musetta's Waltz" from *La Bohème,* Giacomo Puccini

"Prelude to *Te Deum* in D-major," Marc-Antoine Charpentier

"Processional," William Mathias

"Romance no. 2 in F," Ludwig van Beethoven

"Sinfonia" from *Wedding Cantata,* Johann Sebastian Bach

"Sonata for Piano no. 14 in C-sharp minor, op. 27, no. 2,
    Moonlight: 1st movement," Ludwig van Beethoven

"Suite for Orchestra no. 3 in D-major: Air on the G string,"
  Johann Sebastian Bach

"Suite in D-major: Trumpet Voluntary (Prince of Denmark's
  March)," Jeremiah Clarke

"Trumpet Tune," John Stanley

"Trumpet Tune and Air in D," Henry Purcell

"Water Music Suite no. 2: Andante allegro," George Handel

"Wedding March," Felix Alexandre Guilmant

"Wedding March" from *Midsummer Night's Dream,* op. 61, Felix
  Mendelssohn

"Wedding March" from *The Marriage of Figaro,* Wolfgang Amadeus
  Mozart

"Wedding March," from *The Sound of Music*; Richard Rodgers and
  Oscar Hammerstein

Contemporary

"Can't Help Falling in Love," Elvis Presley

"Can You Feel the Love Tonight," Elton John

"Friendship Theme," from *Beaches,* Georges Delerue

"Maybe I'm Amazed," Paul McCartney

"Morning Has Broken," Cat Stevens

"The Prayer," Celine Dion and Andrea Bocelli

"Through the Eyes of Love" (Theme from *Ice Castles*), Melissa
  Manchester

"Unchained Melody," The Righteous Brothers

"When a Man Loves a Woman," Percy Sledge

Additional Ceremony Selections (Vocal or Instrumental)

Traditional / Classical

"Alleluia," Johann Sebastian Bach

"Alleluia from Exsultate Jubilate," Wolfgang Amadeus Mozart

"Amazing Grace," spiritual

"Ave Maria," Franz Schubert

"Concerto for Guitar in D-major: Largo," Antonio Vivaldi

"Dodi Li (My Beloved Is Mine)," Song of Songs

"Hanava Babanot (Beautiful One)," Song of Songs

"In Dulci Jubilo," Hieronymus Praetorius

"Let the Bright Seraphim," George Handel

"Love's Old Sweet Song," James Molloy

"Nearer My God to Thee," Lowell Mason

"Now Thank We All Our God," traditional

"Pastoral Symphony: Pifa," from *Messiah,* George Handel

"Reverie," Claude Debussy

"Rock of Ages," Charles Ives

"Salut D'amour, op. 12," Sir Edward Elgar

"Sheep May Safely Graze," Johann Sebastian Bach

"Songs (4) for Female Voices, 2 Horns and Harp,"
    Johannes Brahms

"The Lord's Prayer," Albert Hay Malotte

"What God Hath Done, Is Rightly Done (from Cantata no. 99),"
    Johannes Sebastian Bach

Contemporary

"All of Me," Billie Holiday or Frank Sinatra

"Cantara," Dead Can Dance

"Evergreen," Barbra Streisand

"In My Life," The Beatles

"She's Got a Way," Billy Joel

"Somewhere," from *West Side Story,* Leonard Bernstein and
    Stephen Sondheim

"That's All," Mel Tormé or Sam Harris

"There Is Love (Wedding Song)," Noel Paul Stookey (versions by
    The Captain & Tennille or Petula Clark)

"True Love," Rebecca St. James

"Watermark," Enya

"We've Only Just Begun," The Carpenters

"You Are So Beautiful," Joe Cocker

"You'll Never Walk Alone," Aretha Franklin

The Recessional

Traditional/Classical

"Agincourt Hymn," John Dunstable

"Alla Hornpipe," from *Water Music Suite no. 2 in D-major,*
    George Handel

"Arrival of the Queen of Sheba," George Handel

"Brandenberg Concerto no. 2," Johann Sebastian Bach

Concerto for Violin in E-major, "Primavera": 1st movement,
    allegro, Antonio Vivaldi

"Cornation March," Sir William Turner Walton

"Grande Choeur Dialogue," Eugene Gigout

"Grand March" from *Aida,* Giuseppe Verdi

"Marche Héroïque," Herbert Brewer

"Music for the Royal Fireworks, no. 4, La Réjouissance," George Handel

"Ode to Joy (Joyful, Joyful, We Adore Thee)" from the Ninth Symphony, Ludwig van Beethoven

"Rejoicing," Georg Telemann

"Rondeau," Henry Purcell

"Sonata in A-major, first movement," Felix Mendelssohn

"Spring," from *The Four Seasons*, Antonio Vivaldi

"Suite de Symphonies no. 1: 1st movement, Rondeau," Jean Joseph Mouret

"Toccata in B-minor," Eugene Gigout

"Transports de Joie (no. 3 from *L'Ascension*)," Olivier Messiaen

"Triumphal March (op. 53, no. 3)," Edvard Grieg

"Trumpet Overture (from *Indian Queen*)," Henry Purcell

"Tuba Tune," Craig Sellar Lang

"We Thank Thee, Lord," Sinfonia in D-major, Canata no. 29, Johann Sebastian Bach

Contemporary

"All You Need Is Love," The Beatles

"Benedictus," Simon and Garfunkel

"Brown Eyed Girl," Van Morrison

"Celebration," Kool & the Gang

"Everlasting Love," Howard Jones

"Finally," CeCe Peniston

"Go There with You," Stephen Curtis Chapman

"Gotta Have Love," Yolanda Adams

"Happy Together," The Turtles

"(I've Had) The Time of My Life," from *Dirty Dancing,* Bill Medley and Jennifer Warnes

"Joy," George Winston

"Let's Face the Music and Dance," Fred Astaire or Diana Krall

"Love Will Keep Us Together," The Captain & Tennille

"Night and Day," Frank Sinatra

Cultural Music and Traditional Instruments

Music is a wonderful way to include your ethnic heritage in your ceremony, too. Incorporate bagpipes, the sitar, the accordion, steel drums, even the banjo or ukulele into your selections. Think about having live musicians at your ceremony site—the drama can't be beat. Another personal idea: include traditional songs from your grandparents' or parents' countries of origin. Don't know where to find these tunes? Ask your elders for their input, and then search the Internet for CDs and local musicians.

The Reception

From cocktails through dinner and dancing the night away, we've got great ideas for your playlist, from old standards to eighties essentials. Of course, this is just the beginning: Your band or DJ's playlist, as well as

Reception:
Questions to Ask Your Musicians and/or DJ

Q: What are some good questions I can ask potential reception musicians or DJs?

A: When you talk to potential reception bands or DJs, ask:

* Do they have a signature sound or style? Does it jibe with what you want? (You may want to ask this when you call to make an appointment; if you want a swing band and this is a blues ensemble, save everyone some time.)

* Does the band or DJ work with a playlist? Can you choose what you want played from it?

* If you want additional selections not on the list, is the band or DJ willing to accommodate you?

* Does/can the bandleader or DJ serve as an MC for the event? Can they also keep quiet, if you prefer that?

* How many band members—i.e., what types of ensembles—are available? If you're talking to a DJ, does he/she work alone, with an assistant, with another DJ, with "dancers" (if you don't want additional entertainment, say so).

* Will the band or DJ bring all their equipment—do you need to supply anything?

* Have they worked at your site before/are they familiar with the acoustics there?

* How much time would they need to set up?

* Do they write breaks into their contract? Would they need meals during the party?

* How many hours does their fee cover? Are there packages? What about overtime costs?

* What do they wear?

Of course, sign a contract with your chosen band/DJ.

your own music collection, will turn up lots of other, perhaps much more personal, ideas.

A caveat: When you're making up your playlist, keep your guests in mind. Maybe you and your fiancé adore Brazilian or ska music, but does Grandma Jean or Uncle George, or even many of your friends? Be sure to keep their tastes in mind as well when you're deciding on your tunes. Yes, it's your day, but you're depending on your guests to keep the dance floor shaking! Consider including a few of your to-die-for tunes—the ones you two just can't live without—and varying the majority of the playlist to accommodate everyone.

Reception Music Notes

- The big question: band or DJ? You may instinctively be leaning toward one or the other—perhaps you love eighties music and just can't picture a wedding band nailing a New Order song, or maybe you just can't fathom a black-tie wedding without a fourteen-piece orchestra. Consider the style of your party: If you want ambience and entertainment, you need a band. If all you care about is serious dancing, go for a DJ. Consider the space: An orchestra needs elbow room. And ultimately, consider your budget: Bands are more expensive, although a great DJ can be pretty pricey, too.

- Consider whether you want to hire a group for cocktails and another for the reception itself (if you will have a traditional luncheon or dinner reception). You could have a jazz combo playing during cocktails, then a DJ for dinner and dancing, or a few members of the reception orchestra playing during cocktails, or the DJ playing background music then.

First Dance Songs

Okay, you only get to choose one first dance song, and we've compiled too many choices! Standards have been performed by multiple artists over the years, so we've selected our favorite renditions; keep in mind that there may be many more versions. Can't decide? Any of these would also be great as dinner or dancing music later on in your reception.

Big Band/Jazz Standards

"A Fine Romance," Joe Derise
"All the Things You Are," Ella Fitzgerald or Tony Bennett

"All the Way," Frank Sinatra or Barry Manilow

"Always," Frank Sinatra or Sarah Vaughan and Billy Eckstine

"As Time Goes By," from *Casablanca,* Tony Bennett or Frank
   Sinatra

"At Last," Etta James

"Baby, I Do," Natalie Cole

"Because of You," Tony Bennett

"Be My Life's Companion," Louis Armstrong or
   Rosemary Clooney

"Body and Soul," Louis Armstrong

"Cheek to Cheek," Ella Fitzgerald or Fred Astaire

First Dance Song Tips

Many couples have "Our Song," and if it's appropriate for a first dance (that is, it's got a beat and you can dance to it!), your choice of first dance may be incredibly easy. But if it's not quite that clear, here are some ways to narrow down your favorite romantic tunes:

- Look through your music collection and pinpoint the albums you both like a lot. Check the song titles. Are there any romantic ones you both really enjoy that you'd feel comfortable dancing to? This doesn't have to be the song that transformed your relationship; it's fine to choose a sweet ditty you just *like*.

- Consider movie soundtracks. There are many "Love Themes from . . ." and if a certain movie really touched both of you, its love theme may be just the song to dance to. If the song is from a movie with a not-so-romantic title, you don't have to count it out—just let your DJ or bandleader know not to mention the name, and avoid something like this: "Barbara and John will now dance their first dance to the theme song from *Dying Young.*"

- Think about whether there's a song that perfectly pertains to your situation: "The Search Is Over" by Survivor if you were friends for a long time before you got together, for example, or "Still the One" by Shania Twain or "Reunited" by Peaches and Herb if you've been together a long time or have otherwise "beat the odds" in your relationship.

- Many standards were performed by multiple artists; we've just listed suggested singers. For example, "You Do Something to Me" is a Cole Porter standard—but did you know that Sinead O'Connor covered it? If you like a certain song, do a search on an Internet CD site for its title to see who's performed it. You might just find the perfect version.

- Would you rather boogie down for your first dance as husband and wife? True, most first dance songs are slow and romantic, but if you want to pick up the pace a bit or do something a little more campy—tango, anyone?—that's fine.

"Come Rain or Come Shine," Billie Holiday or Ray Charles

"Embraceable You," Nat "King" Cole or Frank Sinatra

"Everything I Have Is Yours," Billie Holiday

"From This Moment On," Ella Fitzgerald

"How Do You Speak to an Angel," Dean Martin

"I Can't Give You Anything but Love," Louis Armstrong

"I'm Crazy 'Bout My Baby (And My Baby's Crazy 'Bout Me),"
    Louis Armstrong

"Inseparable," Natalie Cole

"Isn't It Romantic," Frank Sinatra

"It Had to Be You," Harry Connick, Jr., or Frank Sinatra

"It's Love," Lena Horne

"I've Got the World on a String," Bing Crosby or Mel Tormé

"L–O–V–E," Nat "King" Cole

"More," Bobby Darin

"More Than You Know," Billie Holiday

"My Baby Just Cares for Me," Nina Simone

"My One and Only Love," Louis Armstrong or Sting

"My Sweet," Louis Armstrong

"One Moment Worth Years," Louis Armstrong

"Our Day Will Come," Ruby and The Romantics

"Our Love Is Here to Stay," Tony Bennett or Dinah Washington

"Prelude to a Kiss," Ella Fitzgerald or Johnny Mathis

"Someone to Watch Over Me," Etta James or Barbra Streisand

"Tender Is the Night," Tony Bennett

"That Old Black Magic," Mel Tormé or Sarah Vaughan

"The Best Is Yet to Come," Frank Sinatra

"The Man I Love," Billie Holiday or Ella Fitzgerald

"The Nearness of You," Maureen McGovern or Tom Jones

"The Song Is You," Frank Sinatra

"The Sunshine of Your Smile," Frank Sinatra

"The Very Thought of You," Billie Holiday or Nat "King" Cole

"The Way You Look Tonight," Bing Crosby or Frank Sinatra

"We Are in Love," Harry Connick, Jr.

"What Is This Thing Called Love?" Rosemary Clooney or
    Nat "King" Cole

"When I Fall in Love," Nat "King" Cole or Tom Jones

"When Somebody Thinks You're Wonderful," Fats Waller

"You Do Something to Me," Frank Sinatra or Peggy Lee

"You Go to My Head," Tony Bennett or Frank Sinatra

"You're Getting to Be a Habit with Me," Frank Sinatra or
    Mel Tormé

"You're My Thrill," Lena Horne

"You're Nobody Till Somebody Loves You," Dean Martin

"You Send Me," Aretha Franklin or Sam Cooke

"You Stepped Out of a Dream," Sarah Vaughan

Oldies

"A Groovy Kind of Love," The Mindbenders or Phil Collins

"All I Have to Do Is Dream," The Everly Brothers

"Baby, It's You," The Shirelles

"Because," Dave Clark Five

"Born to Be with You," The Chordettes

"Chances Are," Johnny Mathis

"Dedicated to the One I Love," The Shirelles

"Devoted to You," The Everly Brothers

"For the Love of You," The Isley Brothers

"For Your Precious Love," Jerry Butler and The Impressions

"I Love You, Yes I Do," The Platters

"In the Still of the Night," The Five Satins

"I Only Have Eyes for You," The Flamingos or
    Art Garfunkel

"I Only Want to Be with You," Dusty Springfield or
    Vonda Shepard

"Let It Be Me," Nina Simone or the Everly Brothers

"Love Is All Around," The Troggs

"Love Me Tender," Elvis Presley

"Memories Are Made of This," Dean Martin

"My Eyes Adored You," Frankie Valli

"My Girl," The Temptations

"My Own True Love," The Duprees

"Only You," The Platters

"Ooo Baby Baby," Smokey Robinson and The Miracles

"Sea of Love," Phil Phillips and the Twilights or Honeydrippers

"Stand by Me," Ben E. King

"The Look of Love," Dusty Springfield

"To Know Him Is to Love Him," The Teddy Bears

"Warm and Tender Love," Percy Sledge

"You Belong to Me," The Duprees

"You'll Never Walk Alone," Elvis Presley

"(You're My) Soul and Inspiration," The Righteous Brothers

"You Were Made for Me," Sam Cooke

Rock and Pop

"After All," Peter Cetera and Cher

"All I Want Is You," U2

"All My Love," Led Zeppelin

"Always," Atlantic Starr

"Always," Erasure

"And I Love Her," The Beatles

"As Long As You Love Me," Backstreet Boys

"Avalon," Roxy Music

"Babe," Styx

"Baby, Come to Me," James Ingram featuring Patti Austin

"Baby, I Love Your Way," Peter Frampton

"Beautiful Girl," INXS

"Beautiful in My Eyes," Joshua Kadison

"Best of My Love," The Eagles

"Biggest Part of Me," Ambrosia

"Can't Fight This Feeling," REO Speedwagon

"Change the World," Eric Clapton

"Cherish," Kool & the Gang

"Color My World," Chicago

"Come What May," Moulin Rouge

"Completely," Michael Bolton

"Crash Into Me," Dave Matthews Band

"Crazy for You," Madonna

"Crazy Love," Van Morrison

"Don't Know Much," Linda Ronstadt and Aaron Neville

"Don't Know Why," Norah Jones

"Eternal Flame," The Bangles

"Faithfully," Journey

"Falling into You," Celine Dion

"Fields of Gold," Sting

"Forever," Kenny Loggins

"Forever in My Life," Prince

"Giving You the Rest of My Life," Bob Carlisle

"God Must Have Spent a Little More Time on You," 'N Sync

"Have I Told You Lately That I Love You," Van Morrison or Rod Stewart

"Head Over Feet," Alanis Morrisette

"Heaven," Bryan Adams

"Here We Are," Gloria Estefan

"Heroes," David Bowie

"Hold My Hand," Hootie & the Blowfish

"How Much I Feel," Ambrosia

"I Believe in You and Me," Whitney Houston

"Ice Cream," Sarah McLachlan

"I Do (Cherish You)," 98 Degrees

"I Get Weak," Belinda Carlisle

"I Just Wanna Stop," Gino Vannelli

"I Knew I Loved You," Savage Garden

"I'll Always Love You," Taylor Dayne

"I'll Have to Say I Love You in a Song," Jim Croce

"I Love You," Climax Blues Band

"I'm Your Angel," Celine Dion and R. Kelly

"In Your Eyes," Peter Gabriel

"I Remember You," Björk

"It Must Be Love," Madness

"It's All Coming Back to Me Now," Celine Dion

"I Want to Know What Love Is," Foreigner

"I Will," the Beatles

"I Will Always Love You," Whitney Houston

"Just Between You and Me," April Wine

"Just the Way You Are," Billy Joel

"Keep On Loving You," REO Speedwagon

"Kiss Me," Sixpence None the Richer

"Lady," Styx

"Let Love Rule," Lenny Kravitz

"Love Song," Tesla

"Love Song," The Cure

"Make It with You," Bread

"More Than I Can Say," Leo Sayer

"My All," Mariah Carey

"My Love Is Your Love," Whitney Houston

"Never Gonna Let You Go," Sergio Mendes

"Nobody Does It Better," Carly Simon

"No Ordinary Love," Sade

"Nothing's Gonna Change My Love for You," Glenn Medeiros

"Nothing's Gonna Stop Us Now," Starship

"Now That I Found You," Michael Bolton

"On the Wings of Love," Jeffrey Osborne

"Open Arms," Journey

"Save the Best for Last," Vanessa Williams

"She's All I Ever Had," Ricky Martin

"She's an Angel," They Might Be Giants

"Sign Your Name," Terence Trent D'Arby

"Slave to Love," Bryan Ferry

"Somebody," Depeche Mode

"Something in the Way She Moves," James Taylor

"Something So Right," Paul Simon or Annie Lennox

"Stand by My Woman," Lenny Kravitz

"Suddenly," Billy Ocean

"Sweet Thing," Van Morrison

"Take My Breath Away," Berlin

"The Power of Love," Celine Dion

"The Power of Love," Frankie Goes to Hollywood

"Time After Time," Cyndi Lauper

"Time in a Bottle," Jim Croce

"Tonight and Forever," Carly Simon

"Trouble Me," 10,000 Maniacs

"True Companion," Marc Cohn

"Truly," Lionel Richie

"Truly Madly Deeply," Savage Garden

"2 Become 1," Spice Girls

"Vision of Love," Mariah Carey

"Waiting for a Girl Like You," Foreigner

"We Belong," Pat Benatar

"We've Got Tonight," Bob Seger & the Silver Bullet Band

"When I'm with You," Sheriff

"When I Need You," Leo Sayer

"Will You Marry Me?" Vonda Shepard

"Woman," John Lennon

"Wonderful Tonight," Eric Clapton

"Written in the Stars," Elton John and LeAnn Rimes

"You Are the Everything," R.E.M.

"You Give Good Love," Whitney Houston

"You're in My Heart," Rod Stewart

"You're My Best Friend," Queen

"You're My Home," Billy Joel

"You're the Inspiration," Chicago

"Your Love Is King," Sade

"Your Song," Elton John

"You've Made Me So Very Happy," Blood, Sweat & Tears

Motown/R&B/Soul

"Ain't No Mountain High Enough," Ashford & Simpson

"Ain't No Stoppin' Us Now," McFadden & Whitehead

"Ain't Nobody," Chaka Khan

"Ain't Nothing Like the Real Thing," Aretha Franklin

"Ain't No Woman (Like the One I Got)," The Four Tops

"All My Life," K-Ci & Jo Jo

"Always and Forever," Heatwave

"Angel of Mine," Monica

"Back at One," Brian McKnight

"Beautiful," Mary J. Blige

"Being with You," Smokey Robinson

"Best Thing That Ever Happened to Me," Gladys Knight
    & the Pips

"Can't Get Enough of Your Love, Babe," Barry White

"Can't Take My Eyes Off You," Lauryn Hill

"Caught Up in the Rapture," Anita Baker

"Could It Be I'm Falling in Love," the Spinners

"Ebony Eyes," Rick James with Smokey Robinson

"Everything," Mary J. Blige

"Feel Like Makin' Love," Roberta Flack

"Giving You the Best That I've Got," Anita Baker

"Here and Now," Luther Vandross

"I Do It for You (Everything I Do)," Brandy

"I Just Can't Stop Loving You," Michael Jackson

"I'll Be There," The Jackson 5

"I'll Take Care of You," Marvin Gaye

"I.O.U. Me," BeBe & CeCe Winans

"Just the Two of Us," Grover Washington, Jr.

"Kissing You," Keith Washington

"Knocks Me Off My Feet," Stevie Wonder

"Let's Get It On," Marvin Gaye

"Let's Stay Together," Al Green

"Look What You Done for Me," Al Green

"Love and Happiness," Al Green

"My Cherie Amour," Stevie Wonder

"Never Knew Love Like This Before," Stephanie Mills

"Nothing Can Change This Love," Otis Redding

"On Bended Knee," Boyz II Men

"Overjoyed," Stevie Wonder

"Shining Star," the Manhattans

"Since I Fell for You," Al Jarreau

"So Amazing," Luther Vandross

"Solid (As a Rock)," Ashford and Simpson

"So This Is Love," James Ingram

"Spend My Life with You," Eric Benet

"Still," The Commodores

"Sweet Love," Anita Baker

"Sweet Thing," Rufus featuring Chaka Khan

"That's the Way Love Goes," Janet Jackson

"The First Time Ever I Saw Your Face," Roberta Flack

"The Only One for Me," Brian McKnight

"The Sweetest Thing," Lauryn Hill

"This Will Be (An Everlasting Love)," Natalie Cole

"Tonight I Celebrate My Love," Roberta Flack and
    Peabo Bryson

"True Love," Calvin Richardson and Chico DeBarge

"We're in This Love Together," Al Jarreau

"With You I'm Born Again," Billy Preston and Syreeta

"You Are My Lady," Freddie Jackson

"You Make Me Feel Brand New," The Stylistics

"You Mean the World to Me," Toni Braxton

"You're All I Need to Get By," Marvin Gaye and Tami Terrell

"You're Makin' Me High," Toni Braxton

Country

"All I Have," Beth Nelson Chapman

"All I Need to Know," Kenny Chesney

"A Long and Lasting Love," Crystal Gayle

"Amazed," Lonestar

"Darlin' Companion," Johnny Cash and Emmylou Harris

"Feels So Right," Alabama

"Forever and Ever, Amen," Randy Travis

"Friends for Life," Debby Boone

"God Must Have Spent a Little More Time on You," Alabama

"Go There with You," Steven Curtis Chapman

"Grow Old with Me," John Lennon or Mary Chapin Carpenter

"Here, There, and Everywhere," Emmylou Harris

"I Cross My Heart," George Strait

"I Do," Paul Brandt

"If Tomorrow Never Comes," Garth Brooks

"I'll Be There for You," Kenny Rogers

"I'll Still Be Loving You," Restless Heart

"I'll Take Care of You," Dixie Chicks

"I Love the Way You Love Me," John Michael Montgomery

"I Love You," Martina McBride

"In This Life," Colin Raye

"Islands in the Stream," Kenny Rogers and Dolly Parton

"I Swear," John Michael Montgomery

"I Will Always Love You," Dolly Parton

"Love Of My Life," Sammy Kershaw

"Made for Lovin' You," Doug Stone

"Me and You," Kenny Chesney

"No Place That Far," Sara Evans

"Pledging My Love," Emmylou Harris

"She Believes in Me," Kenny Rogers

"Something to Talk About," Bonnie Raitt

"The Man in Love with You," George Strait

"There's No Love Like Our Love," Crystal Gayle and Gary Morris

"The Vows Go Unbroken (Always True to You)," Kenny Rogers

"What a Difference You've Made in My Life," Ronnie Milsap

"When Love Finds You," Vince Gill

Inspired First Dance Choices

"Lady in Red" by Chris DeBurgh—it was the first song we ever danced to together. The bandleader asked me if I wanted him to change the words to "Lady in White," and I said no, but he forgot and changed them for one of the verses anyway!
—Val

Our first dance song was "Friday I'm in Love" by The Cure. Unconventional, but we both loved the song and we married on a Friday, and we are in love, so . . . Our contemporaries loved it, but our parents were a little taken aback by the words ("Wednesday, Thursday, heart attack. . . .").
—Donna

My husband, Mark, and I chose a reggae song by a guy nobody knows called Finley Quaye. We had listened to him endlessly on a vacation in St. John about a year before we got married, and we often sang to and danced with each other to one of his songs called "Your Love Gets Sweeter Every Day." The guests at our wedding looked a little surprised when the band started to play a reggae number for our first dance, but shortly everyone—with or without a partner—was grooving on the dance floor along with us and smiling like crazy.
—Leslie

Believe it or not, my first dance song was "Thank You" by Led Zeppelin. It was my husband's choice—and a precedent setter in our marriage. He's in complete control of our CD collection.
—Monica

Brett and I picked up a Shania Twain CD one day and listened to it in the car. We pulled up to a red light and "From This Moment On" came on. We both fell silent and looked at each other, me with tears in my eyes. We kissed and we just knew that this was our wedding song. The moment was perfect—until people behind us honked because the light had turned green!
—Alison

"You and I," Eddie Rabbitt and Crystal Gayle

"You Decorated My Life," Kenny Rogers

"You're So Beautiful," John Denver

"You're the One," Oak Ridge Boys

"Your Love Amazes Me," John Berry

"You've Got a Way," Shania Twain

From Movies and Shows

"All I Ask of You," from *The Phantom of the Opera,* Andrew Lloyd Webber

"At the Beginning," from *Anastasia,* Richard Marx and Donna Lewis

"A Whole New World" from *Aladdin,* Regina Belle and Peabo Bryson

"Best That You Can Do," from *Arthur,* Christopher Cross

Inspired First Dance Choices

My wife and I chose "Almost Paradise"—it was a hit in the early 1980s, sung by Mike Reno and Ann Wilson. The song had special meaning to us because we were apart for the year preceding our wedding, and we struggled through some very hard times and many obstacles to pull it off.　　**—John**

Our first dance was to Stevie Wonder's "As," which we'd chosen not just for the romantic words, but because it starts out slow and gets faster. As soon as the music picked up we had the DJ tell everyone to join us on the floor. We had instructed certain friends and family (before the wedding) to lead the others in just dancing "freestyle," though Jeff and I continued in the slow dance fashion. It really felt like everyone was dancing in celebration this way, instead of just a mass "couples' dance" to our song.　　**—Amy**

Our first dance song was very unique. We were engaged in Central Park on a rock next to the water where everyone rides rowboats. When we went back to that very spot months later, the Guitar Man of Central Park was performing. There were hundreds of people, but we found a spot on our engagement rock. He started to talk about the most romantic song ever written and how he loved it so much that he included it on his new CD. He started singing "The Way You Look Tonight" and Joe and I just looked at each other. I knew right then that that was our song. We bought his CD a few weeks later, and the Guitar Man of Central Park serenaded us at our wedding.　　**—Dana**

Our first dance song is "This Must Be Heaven" by the R&B group Brainstorm. The song came out in 1976, which is when Ron and I first met—we were in the eighth grade!　　**—Michelle**

"Can You Feel the Love Tonight," from *Lion King*, Elton John

"Can You Read My Mind," from *Superman*, John Williams

"(Everything I Do) I Do It for You," from *Prince of Thieves*,
   Bryan Adams

"Feels Like Home," from *Dawson's Creek*

"Glory of Love," from *Karate Kid II*, Peter Cetera

"I Don't Want to Miss a Thing," from *Armageddon*, Aerosmith

"If I Loved You," from *Carousel*, Richard Rodgers and
   Oscar Hammerstein

"I Finally Found Someone," from *The Mirror Has Two Faces*, Barbra
   Streisand and Bryan Adams

"Love Came for Me," from *Splash*, Placido Domingo

"Love Makes the World Go 'Round," from *Carnival*, Bob Merrill

"Love Theme," from *Superman*, John Williams

"My Heart Will Go On," from *Titanic*, Celine Dion

"Once Upon a Time . . . Story Book Love," from *Princess Bride*,
   Mark Knopfler

"One Hand, One Heart," from *West Side Story*, Leonard Bernstein
   and Stephen Sondheim

"Only You," from *Starlight Express*, Andrew Lloyd Webber and
   Richard Stilgoe

"People Will Say We're in Love," from *Oklahoma*, Richard
   Rodgers and Oscar Hammerstein

"Seasons of Love," from *Rent*, Jonathan Larson

"So in Love," from *Kiss Me, Kate*, Cole Porter

"Someone Like You," from *Jekyll & Hyde*, Frank Wildhorn

"The Last Night of the World," from *Miss Saigon*, Alain Boublil
   and Claude-Michel Schonberg

"They Say It's Wonderful," from *Annie Get Your Gun*, Irving Berlin

"Up Where We Belong," from *An Officer and a Gentleman*,
   Joe Crocker and Jennifer Warnes

"When You Believe," from *Prince of Egypt*, Whitney Houston and
   Mariah Carey

"Why Do I Love You?" from *Showboat*, Jerome Kern and
   Oscar Hammerstein

Reggae

"Baby, I Love Your Way," Big Mountain

"Do It Sweet," Jackie Edwards

"Is This Love," Bob Marley and the Wailers

"Love Me Forever," Dennis Brown

"Love You Baby," Barry Biggs

"Me Love She," Made Cobra and Tricia
"Souls Keep Burning," Dennis Brown
"When I Get Your Love," Chaka Demus and Pilers

Parent Dances

You two may choose to dance with your parents—usually, the bride with her father and/or the groom with his mother. The following are songs appropriate for these dances, but you may choose something completely different that is meaningful to you and your parent for a very personal reason. Or, leave it to your parent to choose the song he or she would enjoy dancing to with you.

"Because You Loved Me," Celine Dion
"Butterfly Kisses," Bob Carlisle
"Come Fly with Me," Frank Sinatra
"Daddy's Hands," Holly Dunn
"Daddy's Little Girl," The Mills Brothers or Al Martino
"Good Riddance," (Time of Your Life), Green Day
"How Sweet It Is (To Be Loved by You)," Marvin Gaye or
    James Taylor
"If I Could," Regina Belle or Nancy Wilson
"I Will Remember You," Sarah McLachlan
"Kind & Generous," Natalie Merchant
"Let Him Fly," Dixie Chicks
"Little Star," Madonna
"Mama," Spice Girls
"Memory," from *Cats,* Andrew Lloyd Webber
"Summer Wind," Frank Sinatra
"Sunrise Sunset," from *Fiddler on the Roof,* Jerry Bock and
    Sheldon Harnick
"Thank Heaven for Little Girls," from *Gigi,* Frederick Loewe and
    Alan Jay Lerner
"The River," Garth Brooks
"The Sweetest Days," Vanessa Williams
"The Times of Your Life," Paul Anka
"The Way We Were," Barbra Streisand
"Think of Me," from *The Phantom of the Opera,* Andrew Lloyd
    Webber
"Through the Years," Kenny Rogers
"Turn Around," Harry Belafonte

"Unforgettable," Nat "King" Cole and/or Natalie Cole
"Wind Beneath My Wings," Bette Midler
"You Are the Sunshine of My Life," Stevie Wonder
"You've Got a Friend," James Taylor

Dinner Music

When it comes to music during the cocktail hour and/or the meal, the main word to keep in mind is *mellow*. Standards and bossa nova are great for this, but there are pop songs that are appropriate, too. Many of the songs on our first dance list and contemporary ceremony music lists would also work. And just about all this dinner music would be great for slow dancing, as well.

Big Band/Jazz Standards

"As Time Goes By," Tony Bennett or
    Engelbert Humperdinck
"Bewitched, Bothered, and Bewildered," Ella Fitzgerald or
    Linda Ronstadt
"Dream a Little Dream of Me," The Mamas and the Papas or
    Dean Martin
"Fly Me to the Moon," Frank Sinatra
"I Get a Kick Out of You," Tony Bennett or Shirley Bassey
"I've Got a Crush on You," Linda Ronstadt
"I've Got My Love to Keep Me Warm," Ella Fitzgerald
"I've Got You Under My Skin," Frank Sinatra
"Misty," Bing Crosby or Johnny Mathis
"One for My Baby," Fred Astaire or Tony Bennett
"Stardust," Harry Connick, Jr., or Nat "King" Cole
" 'Swonderful," Ella Fitzgerald
"That's Amore," Dean Martin
"The Shadow of Your Smile," Frank Sinatra or
    Rosemary Clooney
"The Way You Look Tonight," Frank Sinatra or
    Mel Tormé
"They Can't Take That Away from Me," Ella Fitzgerald and
    Louis Armstrong
"Time After Time," Tony Bennett
"What a Little Moonlight Can Do," Billie Holiday
"You Made Me Love You," Patsy Cline

Oldies/Show Tunes

"Blue Velvet," Bobby Vinton

"Crazy," Patsy Cline

"Fever," Peggy Lee

"Love Me Tender," Elvis Presley

"Moon River," from *Breakfast at Tiffany's,* Henry Mancini

"On the Street Where You Live," from *My Fair Lady,*
  Frederick Loewe and Alan Jay Lerner

"Smoke Gets in Your Eyes," The Platters

"Some Enchanted Evening," from *South Pacific,* Richard Rodgers
  and Oscar Hammerstein

"This Magic Moment," The Drifters

Rock/Pop/R&B

"Alison," Elvis Costello

"Blue," LeAnn Rimes

"Don't Dream It's Over," Crowded House

"Have You Ever Really Loved a Woman?" Bryan Adams

"Holding Back the Years," Simply Red

"I'll Make Love to You," Boyz II Men

"I Second That Emotion," Smokey Robinson & the Miracles

"Moondance," Van Morrison

"Reminiscing," Little River Band

"Smooth Operator," Sade

"True," Spandau Ballet

Bossa Nova/Brazilian

"Aquarela do Brasil," Toots Thielemans and Elis Regina

"Baia," Walter Wanderley

"Corcovado (Quiet Nights of Quiet Stars)," Astrud Gilberto

"Desafinado (Slightly Out of Tune)," Antonio Carlos Jobim or
  Gal Costa

"Girl from Ipanema," Astrud Gilberto or
  Antonio Carlos Jobim

"Más Qué Nada," Tamba Trio or Luis Henrique

"Os Grilos," Marcos Valle

"Triste," Elis Regina

Music
and Dances

Dancing Music: Songs to Get the Party Moving

You'll want great slow and fast tunes to keep the party fresh. Choose smooth grooves from the first dance and dinner music lists to supplement the tripping tunes from the list below. From disco to soul, new wave to rock and roll, don't be afraid to mix it up!

"Addicted to Love," Robert Palmer
"Ain't No Stopping Us Now," McFadden & Whitehead
"Ain't Too Proud to Beg," Temptations
"A Little Respect," Erasure
"All I Wanna Do," Sheryl Crow
"All Shook Up," Elvis Presley
"Another Night," M.C. Sar and The Real McCoy
"Believe," Cher
"Best of My Love," The Emotions
"Bizarre Love Triangle," New Order
"Boogie Oogie Oogie," A Taste of Honey
"Boogie Wonderland," Earth, Wind & Fire
"Boogie Woogie Bugle Boy," Bette Midler
"Born to be Wild," Steppenwolf
"Brick House," The Commodores
"Bring Me Some Water," Melissa Etheridge
"Can't Get Enough of Your Love, Babe," Barry White
"Car Wash," Rose Royce
"Come on, Eileen," Dexy's Midnight Runners
"Conga," Miami Sound Machine
"Crazy," Britney Spears
"Crazy Little Thing Called Love," Queen
"Dance to the Music," Sly & the Family Stone
"Dancing in the Street," Martha Reeves & the Vandellas or David Bowie and Mick Jagger
"Dancing Queen," ABBA
"December, 1963 (Oh, What a Night)," Four Seasons
"Devil Went Down to Georgia," The Charlie Daniels Band
"Disco Inferno," Trammps
"Don't Bring Me Down," Electric Light Orchestra
"Don't Leave Me This Way," Thelma Houston
"Don't Rock the Jukebox," Alan Jackson
"Don't Stop 'Til You Get Enough," Michael Jackson
"Don't You Want Me," Human League
"Doo Wop (That Thing)," Lauryn Hill
"Do You Love Me?" Contours

"Electric Avenue," Eddy Grant

"Enjoy the Silence," Depeche Mode

"Escape (The Piña Colada Song)," Rupert Holmes

"Everybody Have Fun Tonight," Wang Chung

"Every Little Thing She Does Is Magic," The Police

"Fire," Pointer Sisters or Bruce Springsteen

"Freeze Frame," J. Geils Band

"Friends in Low Places," Garth Brooks

"Funkytown," Lipps Inc.

"Genie in a Bottle," Christina Aguilera

"Get Back," The Beatles

"Get Down on It," Kool & the Gang

"Get Down Tonight," KC & the Sunshine Band

"Gettin' Jiggy Wit It," Will Smith

"Gimme Some Lovin'," Steve Winwood

"Gonna Make You Sweat (Everybody Dance Now)," C&C Music
   Factory

"Good Lovin'," Rascals

"Good Times," Chic

"Goody Two Shoes," Adam Ant

"Got to Be Real," Cheryl Lynn

"Groove Is in the Heart," Dee-Lite

"Heart of Glass," Blondie

"Heat Wave," Martha Reeves & the Vandellas

"Holiday," Madonna

"Hot Hot Hot," Buster Poindexter

"Hungry Like the Wolf," Duran Duran

"I Feel Good," James Brown

"I Feel Love," Donna Summer

"If You Had My Love," Jennifer Lopez

"I Knew the Bride (When She Used to Rock and Roll),"
   Nick Lowe

"I Melt with You," Modern English

"I'm Too Sexy," Right Said Fred

"In the Mood," Glenn Miller Orchestra

"Into the Groove," Madonna

"I Say a Little Prayer," Aretha Franklin or Dionne Warwick

"It's the End of the World As We Know It (And I Feel Fine),"
   R.E.M.

"I Want It That Way," Backstreet Boys

"I Will Survive," Gloria Gaynor

"Jamming," Bob Marley

Silly Dances

Come on, you know there's at least one of these that you secretly like! No, you don't have to play all these theme songs at your reception, but one or two may pull some people who otherwise wouldn't be caught dead on the dance floor right out there. Think of the pictures!

"Electric Slide,"
   Marcia Griffiths

"Macarena (Bayside Boys
   Mix)," Los Del Rio

"The Chicken Dance"

"The Hokey Pokey"

"YMCA,"
   Village People

Music
and Dances

"Java Jive," Manattan Transfer or the Ink Spots

"Jump, Jive, an' Wail," Louis Prima or Brian Setzer Orchestra

"Jungle Boogie," Kool & the Gang

"La Bamba," Ritchie Valens

"Last Dance," Donna Summer

"Le Freak," Chic

"Let's Go Crazy," Prince and the Revolution

"Let's Spend the Night Together," Rolling Stones

"Let's Talk About Sex," Salt 'N Pepa

"Life in the Fast Lane," The Eagles

"Light My Fire," The Doors

"Livin' La Vida Loca," Ricky Martin

"Loco-Motion," Kylie Minogue or Grand Funk

"Love Shack," B-52's

Cultural Reception Dances

Many cultures have their own traditional dances of celebration. You may want to include at your reception one that reflects your background or your new spouse's background. To find out more about your culture's dancing customs, ask your parents and grandparents. You'll probably find that the elders in your family are founts of wisdom on this subject!

The Horah This is a traditional Jewish dance that culminates in the bride and groom being raised up on chairs by their peers. If you want to incorporate a lot of traditional Jewish music into your ceremony, consider hiring a klezmer band for the entire party or several hours of it. You can be assured every wedding band can do a rendition of the Horah—it's even becoming popular at non-Jewish weddings.

The Tarantella This dance originated in southern Italy; it's a couple's dance that increases in speed, typically accompanied by castanets and a tambourine.

The Highland Fling This high-energy Scottish dance was supposedly used to test a warrior's strength, stamina, and agility—dance it at your own risk!

The Dollar Dance Polish brides have the pleasure of dancing with many guests—each one pins a dollar to her dress (or puts it in her purse). You can also include the groom in this one; have female guests and relatives dance with and pin money to him. The Polka, with all its varied musical possibilities, is another staple at Polish receptions.

The Tango Want to give your first dance a twist? Include this sensual South American stunner. Think about taking a few tango lessons, then clench that rose between your teeth and get out there!

"Margaritaville," Jimmy Buffett

"Mickey," Toni Basil

"Missing," Everything But the Girl

"Mony Mony," Tommy James & the Shondells or Billy Idol

"Muskrat Ramble," Dukes of Dixieland or Harry Connick, Jr.

"Mustang Sally," Rascals or The Commitments

"My Sharona," The Knack

"Night Fever," Bee Gees

"No Scrubs," TLC

"Now That We Found Love," Heavy D and the Boyz

"Old Time Rock 'n' Roll," Bob Seger & the Silver Bullet Band

"One Love," Bob Marley

"Pink Cadillac," Bruce Springsteen or Southern Pacific

"Pop Muzik," M

"Pretty Woman," Roy Orbison

"Proud Mary," Creedence Clearwater Revival or Ike and
  Tina Turner

"Pump Up the Volume," M|A|R|R|S

"Red Red Wine," UB40

"Relax," Frankie Goes to Hollywood

"Respect," Aretha Franklin

"Rhythm Divine," Enrique Iglesias

"Rhythm of the Night," Debarge

"Rock Around the Clock," Bill Haley and the Comets

"Rockin' at Midnight," Honeydrippers

"Rock This Town," Stray Cats

"Runaround," Blues Traveler

"Save the Last Dance for Me," Tom Jones or The Drifters

"Say You'll Be There," Spice Girls

"(Shake, Shake, Shake) Shake Your Booty," KC & the
  Sunshine Band

"Shake Your Groove Thing," Peaches & Herb

"Should I Stay or Should I Go," the Clash

"Shout," Otis Day & the Knights

"Situation," Yaz

"Start Me Up," Rolling Stones

"Sugarpie Honeybunch," Four Tops

"Superfreak," Rick James

"Superstition," Stevie Wonder

"Sussudio," Phil Collins

"Tainted Love," Soft Cell

"Take the 'A' Train," Duke Ellington or Cab Calloway

AMY AND JEFF

October 3

Lawrence, New York

JEFF, A JAZZ MUSICIAN, and Amy, a graphic designer, wanted to make their ceremony a reflection of themselves. "The music seemed like a logical place to let that happen," Amy says. They decided on two pieces by Charles Mingus, a jazz composer and bassist who recorded from the late forties to the late seventies. "He's always been a favorite of ours," Amy says. For the processional, Amy wanted "Self-Portrait in Three Colors"—"a beautiful, melodic piece." However, it wasn't long enough for everyone to get down the aisle in time, so Jeff wrote a prelude to be played first, nodding to and stylistically introducing the Mingus tune. "He timed it so the prelude played just until after he walked down, and then the Mingus piece started for my maid of honor and then me," says the bride. For the recessional, the couple chose "Reincarnation of a Lovebird," a light, fun piece. Jeff transcribed the music for vibraphone and clarinet, which Laura, a friend of Jeff's from grad school, and Chris, a fellow musician played.

"Tequila," The Champs

"That's the Way (I Like It)," KC & the Sunshine Band

"The Boys of Summer," Don Henley

"The Gambler," Kenny Rogers

"The Hustle," Van McCoy and the Soul City Symphony

"The Twist," Chubby Checker

"This Kiss," Faith Hill

"Try a Little Tenderness," Otis Redding

"Turn the Beat Around," Vickie Sue Robinson or
    Gloria Estefan

"Turn Your Love Around," George Benson

"Twist and Shout," The Beatles

"Twistin' the Night Away," Rod Stewart

"Upside Down," Diana Ross

"Venus," Bananarama or Shocking Blue

"Vogue," Madonna

"Volcano," Jimmy Buffett

"Walking on Sunshine," Katrina and the Waves

"Wannabe," Spice Girls

"We Are Family," Sister Sledge

"We Got the Beat," The Go-Go's

"We Like to Party," Vengaboys

"West End Girls," Pet Shop Boys

"What I Like About You," Romantics

"What You Need," INXS

"Where It's At," Beck

"Who Can It Be Now?" Men at Work

"Woodchopper's Ball," Duke Ellington or Benny Goodman

"(You Make Me Feel Like) A Natural Woman," Aretha Franklin

"You Really Got Me," The Kinks or Van Halen

"You're the First, the Last, My Everything," Barry White

"(Your Love Keeps Lifting Me) Higher and Higher,"
    Jackie Wilson

"You Sexy Thing," Hot Chocolate

"You Shook Me All Night Long," AC/DC

"You Should Be Dancing," The Bee Gees

"You Spin Me Round (Like a Record)," Dead or Alive

"Zoot Suit Riot," Cherry Poppin' Daddies

For more information on music or to submit your
favorite selections, visit www.theknot.com/music

NOTES

NOTES

speeches and toasts

Toasts from family and friends serve as entertainment and, well, an education. The toasting part of your reception is also a time for your guests to get to know you even better through the words of your closest friends and relatives. A room full of loved ones lifting a glass to you and speaking words of affection, recalling funny or touching stories about or moments with the two of you, offering compliments or telling jokes, and generally giving you a warm, fuzzy feeling (watch out for those tearjerker toasts!), can be one of the most memorable and meaningful parts of the party. The traditional toasts and unique ideas in this chapter are meant to inspire you and your wedding party.

Talking Points

- The best man usually serves as toastmaster. The maid of honor can take on this role—or serve as comaster—or she may simply toast the couple right after the best man does. Be sure your honor attendants know that they should lead the toasting.

- Traditionally the groom responds, thanking the best man and toasting his new wife; he may also offer his thanks and appreciation to their parents. These days, the bride also toasts her groom, or with him toasts and thanks their families and their guests.

- Your parents (especially if they are hosting the reception) and other relatives or friends may want to say something, as well.

- Toasts usually happen once everyone has been seated and served drinks, but you may choose to wait do it between courses—after the salad, for example. If either way sounds fine to you, leave it up to your honor attendants.

- While your master of ceremonies (often the bandleader or DJ) may announce to guests that toasting is about to begin, we prefer it if the best man simply goes up to the microphone himself and begins. The traditional way to get people's attention is to clink a wineglass with a utensil. (Of course, guests also clink their glasses at a reception to get the newlyweds to kiss!)

- Make sure the microphone is tested before guests arrive in the reception area. It's nice to avoid all that screeching and awkwardness.

- Ask parents ahead of time whether they're interested in making a toast or speech; let them know you'd love it if they spoke, but they shouldn't feel obligated. Your father, with or without your mother, or even both sets of parents may also make a speech at the very beginning of the reception, before the "official" toasting begins, to

---

ASK CARLEY

Toasting Dos and Don'ts

Q: Are there any rules when it comes to toasting?

A: There are a few etiquette points to be aware of:

- When you're the one being toasted, stay seated, and don't raise your glass.

- If seated, stand when offering a toast, or "take the floor" at a microphone.

- The major players (honor attendants, newlyweds, parents) will probably want to prepare their speech or toast in advance, written out completely or at least in the form of notes. Emotions and nerves can get the best of you otherwise! You may even want to give it a practice run (or two).

- Keep it simple, and keep it personal. Don't try to be a performer if you're not, or use words you normally wouldn't use. Be yourself.

- Brevity is the soul of wit, remember? Even if you have a story to tell, don't use the long version.

- It's fine to drink from a glass of water or other beverage if you are not drinking alcohol; it's more polite than not drinking at all (although some say it's unlucky).

- To "finish" a toast, raise your glass and say the couple's names ("To Jacqueline and Ray"), and take a sip. Everyone else will follow your lead.

- If you're experiencing major stage fright as the bride or groom, remember: Everyone in the room loves you! If you're an honor attendant and don't know everyone in the room, focus on the people you do know and love: the couple. Speak directly to them.

welcome your guests. If they do so, they can still toast you as well at the appropriate time.

- At most Christian and Catholic weddings, a blessing is said before the meal is served; your officiant or a family elder may do the honors. At Jewish weddings, the bride's father says a traditional blessing over the challah bread, which is then torn into pieces and served to every table.

- If you're having a very large wedding, you might want to limit the toasting to just the honor attendants, parents, and you two. Save the stories and anecdotes for the more casual atmosphere of the rehearsal dinner or a postwedding brunch.

- That said, marathon toasting sessions have turned into a bit of a wedding trend. If you do want many people to be able to toast, maybe break it up into a few shorter sessions during the cocktail hour, during dinner, and during the cake cutting.

- If there are kids involved (from a first marriage, etc.), offer them a chance to toast, or make sure to remember to toast them.

- Use the toasting ideas in this chapter as a starting point. You can integrate words into your own original speech ("As Voltaire said . . ."; "In the words of Willa Cather . . . "), giving them the significance you choose by relating them to the person or people you're toasting. The idea is to make everyone in the room feel the universal—and therefore personal—importance of the words.

Traditional and Cultural Toasts

May the road rise to meet you.
May the wind be always at your back,
the sun shine warm upon your face,
the rain fall soft upon your fields,
and until we meet again
may God hold you in the hollow of His hand.

—Irish blessing

Ten thousand things bright
Ten thousand miles, no dust
Water and sky one color
Houses shining along your road.

—Chinese blessing

Ka mau ki aha. (May you never thirst again.)

—Traditional Hawaiian wedding toast

A toast to love and laughter,
and happily ever after.

—Traditional toast

May you grow old on one pillow.

—Armenian blessing

Where there is love there is no sin.

—Montenegrin proverb

When the husband drinks to the wife,
all would be well; when the wife drinks
to the husband, all is.

—English proverb

May their joys be as bright as the
morning, and their sorrows but shadows
that fade in the sunlight of love.

—Armenian blessing

Happy the bride and bridegroom and
thrice happy are they whose love
grows stronger day by day and whose
union remains undissolved until the
last day.

—African-American blessing

May your love be like the misty rain,
gentle coming in but flooding the river.

—African blessing

May your love be as endless as your
wedding rings.

—Traditional blessing

Marriage has teeth, and him bit very hot.

—Jamaican proverb

May their joys be as deep as the ocean
And their misfortunes as light as the foam.

—Armenian blessing

Love is like a baby;
it needs to be treated gently.

> —*Congolese proverb*

Ad multos annos—to many years!

> —*Latin toast*

Deep love is stronger than life.

> —*Jewish proverb*

Try to reason about love and you will lose
your reason.

> —*French proverb*

Love and eggs are best when they are
fresh.

> —*Russian proverb*

Let's drink to love, which is nothing—
unless it's divided by two.

> —*Irish blessing*

Here's to the bride and the groom!
May you have a happy honeymoon,
May you lead a happy life,
May you have a bunch of money soon,
And live without all strife.

> —*Traditional toast*

Here's to the groom with bride so fair,
And here's to the bride with groom so rare!

> —*Traditional toast*

Here's to the husband
And here's to the wife;
May they remain
Lovers for life.

> —*Traditional toast*

May your joys be as sweet as spring flowers that grow.
As bright as a fire when winter winds blow,
As countless as leaves that float down in the fall,
As serene as the love that keeps watch over us all.

> —*Old English blessing*

The heart that loves is always young.

—Greek proverb

Insomuch as love grows in you, so beauty grows. For love is the beauty of the soul.

—St. Augustine

Let us toast the health of the bride;
Let us toast the health of the groom,
Let us toast the person that tied;
Let us toast every guest in the room.

—Traditional toast

Blessings

Be present at our table, Lord.
Be here and everywhere adored.
Those mercies bless, and grant that we
May feast in Paradise with Thee.

—John Cennick

The Lord bless you and keep you!
The Lord let his face shine upon you,
and be gracious to you!
The Lord look upon you kindly and give you peace!

—Numbers 6:24–26

Bless, O Lord, this food to our use, and us to
Thy service, and make us ever needful of the
needs of others, in Jesus' name. Amen.

—Traditional Protestant grace

Bless us, O Lord, and these Thy gifts
which we have received out of Thy
bounty, through Christ Our Lord. Amen.

—Traditional Catholic grace

For what we are about to receive, the Lord make
    us truly thankful, for Christ's sake. Amen.
What we are about to receive, may the Trinity
    and the Unity bless. Amen.

—Grace before meal

Barukh atah Adonai Elohaynu melekh ha-olam ha-motzi lechem min ha-aretz. Blessed are You, Adonai our God, Source of the Universe, who brings forth bread from the earth. Amen.

> —*Traditional Jewish blessing over challah bread (*Ha-Motzi*)*

All love should be simply stepping stones to the love of God. . . . Blessed be His name for His great goodness and mercy.

> —*Plato*

Shakespearean Toasts and Blessings

A flock of blessings light upon thy back.

> —Romeo and Juliet, *Act III*

Fair thought and happy hours attend on you.

> —The Merchant of Venice, *Act III*

Look down you gods,
And on this couple drop a blessed crown.

> —The Tempest, *Act V*

I wish you all the joy you can wish.

> —The Merchant of Venice, *Act III*

The best of happiness, honor, and fortunes keeps with you.

> —Timon of Athens, *Act I*

God, the best maker of all marriages,
Combine your hearts in one.

> —King Henry V, *Act V*

Love comforteth like sunshine after rain.

> —*from "Venus and Adonis"*

Honor, riches, marriage-blessing,
Love continuance, and increasing,
Hourly joys be still upon you!
Juno sings her blessings on you.

> —The Tempest, *Act IV*

Toasts for Members of the Wedding Party

We've organized the following toast ideas by wedding-party members whom we felt they would be appropriate for, but the list is not at all set in stone. Feel free to borrow from any section, no matter what your role in the wedding. The most important thing is that the words you choose to use contain the sentiment you want to convey. You'll want to speak personally for most of your toast, but these traditional toasts and sayings are wonderful to use when raising your glass when you come to a close, or as an introduction if you're trying to make a point about the couple's relationship that the quote embodies.

From Best Man

Those who have both true love and true
friendship have received the highest gift
God can offer.

—Anonymous

May you look back on the past with as much
pleasure as you look forward to the future.

—Irish toast

May you live as long as you want and
want nothing as long as you live.

—Traditional toast

Here's to health, peace, and prosperity;
May the flower of love never be nipped by the
    frost of disappointment;
Nor shadow of grief fall among a member of
    this circle.

—Irish toast

A health to you,
A wealth to you,
And the best that life can give to you.
May fortune still be kind to you.
And happiness be true to you,
And life be long and good to you,
Is the toast of all your friends to you.

—Irish toast

Cool breeze
Warm fire
Full moon
Easy chair
Empty plates
Soft words
Sweet songs
Tall tales
Short sips
Long life.

—*John Egerton*

Love is born with the pleasure of looking
at each other, it is fed with the necessity
of seeing each other, it is concluded with
the impossibility of separation.

—*Jose Martí*

May the hinges of the friendship never
rust, nor the wings of love lose a feather.

—*Allan Ramsay, from "Reminiscences of Scottish Life"*

Marriage is the most natural state of man,
and the state in which you will find solid
happiness.

—*Benjamin Franklin*

I believe that love cannot be bought
except with love, and he who has a good
wife wears heaven in his hat.

—*John Steinbeck*

You have to walk carefully in the
beginning of love; the running across
fields into your lover's arms can only
come later, when you're sure they won't
laugh if you trip.

—*Jonathan Carroll,* Outside the Dog Museum

Never do anything in the first year of
your married life that you do not want to
do for the rest of your life.

—*Naomi Fuller Worsley*

LAURIE & CHRIS

July 13

Falmouth, Massachusetts

THOUGH THEY HAD BEEN ACQUAINTANCES since meeting freshman year at Harvard University, it was their postgraduation political jobs in Washington, D.C., that initiated a lasting friendship—and nothing more—for nearly a decade. Many years later, Laurie Kohn, a thirty-four-year-old visiting professor of law at Georgetown University, and Chris Murphy, a thirty-four-year-old executive director of City Year, tied the knot at Bourne Farm on Cape Cod.

Because they wanted their guests to feel free to mingle and dance, sans interruption, they invited any friends or family who wanted to give toasts to speak at the rehearsal dinner instead of at the wedding. Taking the lead was Laurie's father. "He wrote a 'song book' for us and we had a sing-along," remembers Laurie. "He had taken popular tunes and rewritten the words based on my life with Chris. This is a long-time Kohn family tradition."

However, the wedding day would not have been complete without a few moments of heartfelt congratulations. Select family members and friends were allowed "speech time." As people entered the dinner tent, Laurie's mother and father each gave a welcome speech. Chris's mother and father followed with toasts of their own, including traditional Irish blessings given in light of the groom's heritage. Between the first and the main courses, Chris's closest friend and Laurie's best friend from college both spoke. Between the main course and dessert, Chris's brother, Chip, and Laurie's sister and brother-in-law said the last words. "Chip wrote an epic poem for the wedding," laughs Laurie about the witty and even politically angled rhyme.

> When I was old enough to think, my brother became so influential.
> He was eight years older than me and I knew so full of potential . . .
> So I decided to set out and think long hard about what I could say.
> After all, he is my perfect brother, and this is his perfect day! . . .
> You've found your perfect match,
> And let me tell you, she sure is a catch.
> And in addition to being all this, and definitely all that,
> I thank God the most, she isn't a Republican, but a Democrat.

After dessert, Chris and Laurie offered a champagne toast and thanked everyone for coming by pointing out that nobody was at the wedding "randomly" but that each person was invited because he or she had played an important role in their lives. Chris then toasted Laurie by admitting that just maybe he *had* had romantic feelings for her during their ten-year platonic friendship.

The Knot Guide
to Wedding Vows
and Traditions

154

Everything comes to us from others. To
be is to belong to someone.

    —*Jean-Paul Sartre*

There is no possession more valuable than
a good and faithful friend.

    —*Socrates*

Marriage is our last, best chance to grow up.

    —*Joseph Barth*

To keep your marriage brimming, with love in
the wedding cup, whenever you're wrong,
admit it; whenever you're right, shut up.

    —*Ogden Nash*

As soon as you cannot keep anything
from a woman, you love her.

    —*Paul Geraldy*

The loving are the daring.

    —*Bayard Taylor*

The most precious possession that ever comes
to a man in this world is a woman's heart.

    —*Josiah Gilbert Holland*

Who, being loved, is poor?

    —*Oscar Wilde*

In marriage do thou be wise: Prefer the
person before money, virtue before
beauty, the mind before the body; then
thou hast a wife, a friend, a companion,
a second self.

    —*William Penn*

To the newlyweds: May "for better or worse"
    be far better than worse.
May the most you ever wish for be the least
    you ever receive.
May the saddest day of your future be no worse
Than the happiest day of your past.

    —*Traditional toast*

From Maid of Honor

May there always be work for your hands to do.
May your purse always hold a coin or two.
May the sun always shine on your windowpane.
May a rainbow be certain to follow each rain.
May the hand of a friend always be near you.
May God fill your heart with gladness to cheer you.

   —Irish toast

May your hands be forever clasped in friendship
and your hearts joined forever in love.

   —Anonymous

May the rocks in your field turn to gold.

   —Irish blessing

Love is not finding someone to live with,
it's finding someone you can't live
without.

   —Rafael Ortiz

All love is sweet, given or returned . . .
Those who inspire it most are fortunate . . .
But those who feel it most are happier still.

   —Percy Bysshe Shelley

In a great romance, each person plays a
part the other really likes.

   —Elizabeth Ashley

The capacity to love is tied to being able
to be awake, to being able to move out of
yourself and be with someone else in a
manner that is not about your desire to
possess them, but to be with them, to be
in union and communion.

   —bell hooks

Love remains a secret even when spoken,
for only a true lover truly knows that he
is loved.

   —Rabindranath Tagore

Anyone can be passionate, but it takes real
lovers to be silly.

—*Rose Franken*

We cannot really love anybody with
whom we never laugh.

—*Agnes Repplier*

There is no more lovely, friendly, and
charming relationship, communion, or
company than a good marriage.

—*Martin Luther*

Let anniversaries come and let
anniversaries go—but may your
happiness continue on forever.

—*Anonymous*

Here's to marriage, that happy estate that
resembles a pair of scissors: So joined that
they cannot be separated, often moving in
opposite directions, yet punishing anyone
who comes between them.

—*Sidney Smith*

And this is my prayer: that your love may
abound more and more in knowledge and
depth of insight.

—*Philippians 1:9*

True friendship comes when silence
between two people is comfortable.

—*Dave Tyson Gentry*

The time to be happy is now;
the place to be happy is here.

—*Robert G. Ingersoll*

Infatuation is when you think that he's as
sexy as Robert Redford, as smart as
Henry Kissinger, as noble as Ralph
Nader, as funny as Woody Allen, and as
athletic as Jimmy Connors. Love is when
you realize that he's as sexy as Woody

Allen, as smart as Jimmy Connors, as funny as Ralph Nader, as athletic as Henry Kissinger, and nothing like Robert Redford—but you'll take him anyway.

—*Judith Viorst*

Any time that is not spent on love is wasted.

—*Torquato Tasso*

Here's to the health of the happy pair;
May good luck follow them everywhere;
And may each day of wedded bliss
Be always as sweet and joyous as this.

—*Traditional toast*

For where the heart is, that is sure to be where your treasure is.

—*Matthew 6:21*

We never live so intensely as when we love strongly. We never realize ourselves so vividly as when we are in full glow of love for others.

—*Walter Rauschenbusch*

Never is true love blind, but rather brings an added light.

—*Phoebe Cary*

Keep love in your heart. A life without it is like a sunless garden when the flowers are dead. The consciousness of loving and being loved brings a warmth and richness to life that nothing else can bring.

—*Oscar Wilde*

Life is only life forevermore
Together wing to wing and oar to oar.

—*Robert Frost*

To love someone deeply gives you strength. Being loved by someone deeply gives you courage.

—*Lau Tzu*

Love is like a mirror. When you love
another you become his mirror and he
becomes yours. . . . And reflecting each
other's love you see infinity.

   —*Leo Buscaglia,* Love

There is nothing more lovely in life than
the union of two people whose love for
one another has grown through the years
from the small acorn of passion into a
great rooted tree.

   —*Vita Sackville-West*

Love, be true to her; Life, be dear to her;
Health, stay close to her; Joy, draw near to her;
Fortune, find what you can do for her,
Search your treasure-house through and through for her,
Follow her footsteps the wide world over—
And keep her husband always her lover.

   —*Anna Lewis, "To the Bride"*

Love is like quicksilver in the hand. Leave
the fingers open and it stays. Clutch it,
and it darts away.

   —*Dorothy Parker*

From Parents

When children find true love,
parents find true joy.
Here's to your joy and ours, from this day forward.

   —*Anonymous*

The way to Happiness:
Keep your heart free from hate,
Your mind from worry.
Live simply. Expect little. Give much.

   —*Traditional saying*

Be ye kind to one another.

   —*Ephesians 4:32*

Love one another and you will be happy.
It's as simple and as difficult as that.

—*Michael Leunig*

A good marriage is at least 80 percent
good luck in finding the right person at
the right time. The rest is trust.

—*Nanette Newman*

If you are considering marriage, ask
yourself one question: Will I still enjoy
talking with her when I'm old?

—*Friedrich Nietzsche*

Chains do not hold a marriage
together. It is threads, hundreds of tiny
threads which sew people together
through the years. That is what makes
a marriage last.

—*Simone Signoret*

Success in marriage depends on being
able, when you get over being in love, to
really love. . . . You never know anyone
until you marry them.

—*Eleanor Roosevelt*

The great secret of a successful marriage
is to treat all disasters as incidents and
none of the incidents as disasters.

—*Sir Harold Nicolson*

Love and work are the cornerstones of
our humanness.

—*Sigmund Freud*

Love does not dominate; it cultivates.

—*Johann Wolfgang von Goethe*

Love is blind—marriage is the eye-opener.

—*Pauline Thomason*

The first duty of love is to listen.

—*Paul Tillich*

There is no remedy for love but to
love more.

—*Henry David Thoreau*

Immature love says: "I love you because I
need you." Mature love says: "I need you
because I love you."

—*Erich Fromm*

It is wrong to think that love comes
from long companionship and
persevering courtship. Love is the
offspring of spiritual affinity, and
unless that affinity is created in a
moment, it will not be created for
years or even generations.

—*Kahlil Gibran*

Love is everything it's cracked up to be.
That's why people are so cynical about it.
It really is worth fighting for, being brave
for, risking everything for. And the
trouble is, if you don't risk anything,
you risk even more.

—*Erica Jong*

Marriage is an edifice that must be rebuilt
every day.

—*André Maurois*

The story of a love is not important—
what is important is that one is capable of
love. It is perhaps the only glimpse we are
permitted of eternity.

—*Helen Hayes*

The man or woman you really love will
never grow old to you. Through the
wrinkles of time, through the bowed
frame of years, you will always see the
dear face and feel the warm heart union
of your eternal love.

—*Alfred A. Montapert*

You will find as you look back upon your
life that the moments when you have
truly lived are the moments when you
have done things in the spirit of love.

—Henry Drummond

Everyone admits that love is wonderful and
necessary, yet no one agrees on just what it is.

—Diane Ackerman

The only way of full knowledge lies in
the act of love; this act transcends
thought, it transcends words. It is the
daring plunge into the experience of
union. To love somebody is not just a
strong feeling—it is a decision, it is a
judgment, it is a promise.

—Erich Fromm, The Art of Loving

Whatever you do, love those who love you.

—Voltaire

A successful marriage requires falling in love
many times, always with the same person.

—Mignon McLaughlin

When angry, count to a hundred.

—Mark Twain

Age does not protect you from love,
but love to some extent protects you
from age.

—Jeanne Moreau

Love consists in this: That two solitudes
protect and touch and greet each other.

—Rainer Maria Rilke, Letters to a Young Poet

A generation of children on the children
of your children.

—Irish blessing

Grandchildren are the crown of old men,
And the glory of sons is their fathers.

—Proverbs 17:6

You don't marry one person; you marry
three—the person you think they are, the
person they are, and the person they are
going to become as the result of being
married to you.

—Richard Needham

May you have enough happiness to
    keep you sweet;
enough trials to keep you strong;
enough sorrow to keep you human;
enough hope to keep you happy;
enough failure to keep you humble;
enough success to keep you eager;
enough friends to give you comfort;
enough faith and courage in yourself,
    your business, and your country to
    banish depression;
enough wealth to meet your needs;
enough determination to make each day
    a better day than yesterday.

—Traditional blessing
(feel free to make up your own additional points)

The more that you love one another, the
closer you will come to God.

—*Traditional saying*

Without understanding, your love is not
true love. You must look deeply in order to
see and understand the needs, aspirations,
and suffering of the one you love.

—*Thich Nhat Hanh,* The Heart of the Buddha's Teaching

A family starts with a young man falling
in love with a girl. No superior
alternative has been found.

—*Winston Churchill*

Coming together is a beginning;
Keeping together is progress;
Working together is success.

—*Henry Ford*

Never go to bed angry. Stay up and fight.

—*Phyllis Diller*

When in doubt, tell the truth.

—*Mark Twain*

Don't smother each other. No one can
grow in shade.

—*Leo Buscaglia*

There is no secret to a long marriage—it's
hard work. . . . It's serious business, and
certainly not for cowards.

—*Ossie Davis*

Be of love (a little) more careful than of
anything.

—*E. E. Cummings*

The secret of health, happiness, and long life: If
you simply learn how to accept and express
love, you will live longer . . . be happier . . .
grow healthier. For love is a powerful force.

—*Alfred A. Montapert*

May I wish for you the knowledge . . . that
marriages do not Take Place, they are made by
hand; that there is always an element of
discipline involved; that however perfect the
honeymoon, the time will come, however brief
it is, when you will wish she would fall
downstairs and break a leg. This goes for her,
too. But the mood will pass, if you give it time.

—*Raymond Chandler*

From Siblings and/or Adult Children

Love does not consist in gazing at each other,
but in looking outward together in the same direction.

—*Antoine de Saint-Exupéry*

May you have warm words on a cold evening,
A full moon on a dark night,
And the road downhill all the way to your door.

—*Irish blessing*

There is no surprise more magical than
the surprise of being loved. It is God's
finger on man's shoulder.

—*Charles Morgan*

Love is not a matter of counting the years, it
is making the years count. Love is the master
key that opens the gates of happiness.

—*Oliver Wendell Holmes*

To get the full value of a joy you must
have somebody to divide it with.

—*Mark Twain*

If it is your time, love will track you
down like a cruise missile.

—*Lynda Barry*

When you love someone all your saved-
up wishes start coming out.

—*Elizabeth Bowen*

Love is love's reward.

—*John Dryden*

Only the complete person can love.

—*Confucius*

When love and skill work together,
expect a masterpiece.

—*John Ruskin*

Our affections are our life. We live by
them; they supply our warmth.

—*Anonymous*

To your coming anniversaries—may they
be outnumbered only by your coming
pleasures.

—*Anonymous*

What greater thing is there for two
human souls than to feel that they are
joined . . . to strengthen each other . . .
to be at one with each other in silent
unspeakable memories.

—*George Eliot*

May your hands be forever clasped in
friendship and your hearts joined forever
in love.

—*Traditional blessing*

A happy marriage perhaps represents the
ideal of human relationship—a setting in
which each partner, while acknowledging
the need of the other, feels free to be what
he or she by nature is: a relationship in
which instinct as well as intellect can find
expression; in which giving and taking are
equal; in which each accepts the other.

—*Anthony Storr*

A life lived in love will never be dull.

—*Leo Buscaglia*

May you be poor in misfortune
Rich in blessings
Slow to make enemies
And quick to make friends.
But rich or poor, quick or slow,
May you know nothing but happiness
From this day forward.

　　—*Traditional blessing*

Though weary, love is not tired;
Though pressed, it is not straitened;
Though alarmed, it is not confounded.
Love securely passes through all.

　　—*Thomas à Kempis*

Where there is great love,
there are always wishes.

　　—*Willa Cather*

From Bride to Groom

If ever two were one, then surely we.
If ever man were lov'd by wife, then thee;
If ever wife was happy in a man,
Compare with me, ye women, if you can.
I prize thy love more than whole mines of gold,
Or all the riches that the East doth hold.
My love is such that rivers cannot quench,
Nor ought but love from thee, give recompense.
Thy love is such I can no way repay,
The heavens reward thee manifold, I pray.
Then while we live, in love let's so persever
That when we live no more, we may live ever.

　　—*Anne Bradstreet, "To My Dear and Loving Husband"*

If I know what love is, it is because of you.

　　—*Hermann Hesse*

Yet everything that touches us, me and you,
takes us together like a violin's bow,
which draws *one* voice out of two separate strings.

If you're nervous, tossing in a funny anecdote or joke can break the ice and make you feel more comfortable—and what's better than cracking up an audience? Some famous humorists to check out for droll inspiration: Mark Twain, Jane Austen, Oscar Wilde, Dorothy Parker, and Shakespeare. Be sure not to miss quotes from deadpan celebrities like Woody Allen ("I tended to place my wife under a pedestal") and Mae West ("Marriage is a great institution, but I'm not ready for an institution"). Or look into the newspaperly writings of Dave Barry, Ann Landers, Dear Abby, and Erma Bombeck.

Upon what instrument are we two spanned?
And what musician holds us in his hand?
Oh, sweetest song.

> —*Rainer Maria Rilke, from "Love Song,"*
> *translated by Stephen Mitchell*

The minute I heard my first love story
I started looking for you, not knowing
how blind that was.

Lovers don't finally meet somewhere.
They're in each other all along.

> —*Rumi, "The Minute I Heard,"*
> *translated by Coleman Barks with John Moyne*

Because I love you truly,
Because you love me, too,
My very greatest happiness
Is sharing life with you.

> —*Minna Thomas Antrim*

My bounty is as boundless as the sea,
My love as deep; the more I give to thee,
The more I have, for both are infinite.

> —*William Shakespeare,* Romeo and Juliet, *Act II (spoken by Juliet)*

Love is what you've been through
with somebody.

> —*James Thurber*

May we love as long as we live,
and live as long as we love.

> —*Anonymous*

To love a person means to agree
to grow old with him.

> —*Albert Camus*

Your words dispel all of the care in the world and make me happy. . . . They are as necessary to me now as sunlight and air. . . . Your words are my food, your breath my wine—you are everything to me.

> —*Sarah Bernhardt*

Your life and my life flow into each other as wave
flows into wave, and unless there is peace and joy
and freedom for you, there can be no real peace or
joy or freedom for me. To see reality—not as we
expect it to be but as it is—is to see that unless we
live for each other and in and through each other,
we do not really live very satisfactorily; that there
can really be life only where there really is, in just
this sense, love.

   —Frederick Buechner, The Magnificent Defeat

With one glance
I loved you
With a thousand hearts.

   —Mihri Hatun, from "At One Glance," translated by Talat S. Halman

Come the wild weather,
come sleet or come snow,
We will stand by each other,
however it blow.

   —Simon Dach

Our kindred spirits love and are loved like
the sun and moon shining in together
from all sides.

   —Turkish saying

My sweetheart
a long time
I have been waiting for you
to come over
where I am.

   —Chippewa song

My fellow, my companion, held most dear,
My soul, my other self, my inward friend.

   —Mary Sidney Herbert

Love me, sweet, with all thou art,
Feeling, thinking, seeing, —
Love me in the lightest part,
Love me in full being.

   — Elizabeth Barrett Browning, from "A Man's Requirements"

What Did You Just Say?

What's toasting appropriate:

- Beginning by saying you are honored to be here to share the wedding day with the couple.

- Talking casually about your relationship with the bride and/or groom (what it is, when you met) and relating one or two quick anecdotes.

- Pointing out what's special about their relationship and why you think they're perfect for each other.

- Offering gentle advice about marriage or love, from your own experience.

What's not:

- Dwelling on potentially touchy subjects, like a difference in religion or race, or an unhappy ex-spouse.

- Apologizing for being a bad speaker, or saying you didn't really want to speak.

- Talking too much about the bride's or groom's past conquests (you may do so in a short and sweet, harmless way).

- Being cryptic (don't tell stories that only the bride and groom will understand; you'll lose your audience).

- Talking for too long—try not to go over five minutes, tops.

- Fidgeting or clearing your throat (if you feel dry, keep a glass of water close by and take a quick sip before you begin talking).

I am not sure that Earth is round
Nor that the sky is really blue.
The tale of why the apples fall
May or may not be true.
I do not know what makes the tides
Nor what tomorrow's world may do,
But I have certainty enough,
For I am sure of you.

—Amelia Josephine Burr

His mouth is sweetness itself;
he is all delight.
Such is my lover, and such my friend,
O daughters of Jerusalem.

—Song of Solomon

We are custodians, keeper of each
other's hearts and secrets. We treasure
them with tenderness and fidelity. There
is always risk when one is dealing with
priceless treasures. But we . . . prefer to
take that risk.

>   —*Lionel A. Whiston,* For Those We Love

From Groom to Bride

Drink to me only with thine eyes,
And I will pledge with mine;
Or leave a kiss within the cup,
And I'll not look for wine.

>   —*Ben Jonson, from "Song: To Celia (II)"*

Grow old along with me!
The best is yet to be.

>   —*Robert Browning*

Wherever I roam, whatever realms I see,
My heart untravelled fondly returns to thee.

>   —*Oliver Goldsmith*

Just to see her was to love her,
Love but her, and love forever.

>   —*Robert Burns*

When the heart is full, the tongue
cannot speak.

>   —*Scottish proverb*

You are all-beautiful, my beloved,
and there is no blemish in you.

>   —*Song of Solomon*

I have spread my dreams under your feet;
Tread softly, because you tread on my dreams.

>   —*William Butler Yeats*

The hours I spend with you I look upon
as sort of a perfumed garden, a dim
twilight, and a fountain singing to it . . .

you and you alone make me feel that
I am alive. . . . Other men it is said have
seen angels, but I have seen thee, and
thou art enough.

—*George Moore*

If I were to lose everything I had worked
for in life all at once . . . As long as I still
had you I would feel as if I were the
richest man in the world.

—*Michael Wheeler*

Doubt thou that the stars are fire;
Doubt that the sun doth move;
Doubt truth to be a liar;
But never doubt I love.

—*William Shakespeare,* Hamlet, *Act II*

I have spread no snares today;
I am caught in my love of you.

—*Egyptian saying*

She walks in Beauty, like the night
Of cloudless climes and starry skies;
And all that's best of dark and bright
Meet in her aspect and her eyes:
Thus mellowed to that tender light
Which Heaven to gaudy day denies.

—*Lord Byron, from "She Walks in Beauty"*

I love you,
Not only for what you are,
But for what I am
When I am with you.
I love you,
Not only for what
You have made of yourself
But for what you are making of me.

—*Roy Crots*

Soft lips, can I tempt you to an eternity
of kissing?

—*Ben Jonson*

Here is to loving, to romance, to us.
May we travel together through time.
We alone count as none, but together we're one.
For our partnership puts love to rhyme.

—*Irish blessing*

Thou art the star that guides me
Along life's changing sea;
And whatever fate betides me,
This heart still turns to thee.

—*George P. Morris*

Each shining light about us
Has its own peculiar grace,
But every light of heaven
Is in my darling's face.

—*John Hay*

Love not me for comely grace
For my pleasing eye or face,
Nor for any outward part,
No, nor for my constant heart;
For those may fail or turn to ill,
So thou and I shall sever;
Keep therefore a true woman's eye,
And love me still, but know not why.
So hast thou the same reason still
To dote upon me ever.

—*Anonymous*

Give me a kiss, and to that kiss a score;
Then to that twenty, add a hundred more;
A thousand to that hundred; so kiss on,
To make that thousand up a million;
Treble that million, and when that is done,
Let's kiss afresh, as when we first begun.

—*Robert Herrick, from "Hesperides"*

It warms me, it charms me,
To mention but her name,
It heats me, it beats me,
And sets me heart on flame.

—*Robert Burns*

The Last Word

Here are toasting words from around the world. All translate to "To your health," unless otherwise noted.

Cheers!—English, Australian

A votre santé!—French

Salud!—Spanish, Mexican, Latin American

Salud, pesetas, y amor . . . y tiempo para gozarlos! (Health, money, and love . . . and time to enjoy them!) —Spanish

Salute! or *Cin Cin!* (All things good for you!) —Italian

Prosit!—Austrian, German

Za vashe zdorovia! —Russian

Kanpai! (Bottoms up/Dry glass!) or *Banzai!* (Our last farewell!)—Japanese

Kanpei! (Dry glass!) —Chinese

L'chaim! (To life!) or *Mazel tov!* (Congratulations!) —Jewish

Slainte!—Scottish/Gaelic

Stin ygia sou! or *Oopa!* (Hooray!)—Greek

Chai yo!—Thai

Chu kha ham ni da! (Congratulations!)—Korean

Skal!—Scandinavian

Kou ola kino! or *Hauoli maoli oe!* (To your happiness!)—Hawaiian

Aap ki sehat ke liye! —Indian (Hindu)

Speeches
and Toasts

173

JESSICA AND BYRON

September 27

Hawley, Pennsylvania

WEDDING RECEPTION GUESTS often clink their glasses with utensils to get the newlyweds to share a kiss. But Jessica and Byron, fresh from exchanging their vows in Hawaii and back in Pennsylvania (Jessica's home state) to celebrate with family and friends, would have none of that. "The only way we'd kiss was if an entire table got up and sang, in unison, a song with the word *love* in it," Jessica says. The couple were serenaded with such campy tunes as "The Love Boat Theme" and "Love Stinks" by the J. Geils Band, but the most touching moment was when the mother of the bride stood and led her table in a rendition of "Rainbow Connection" (which includes the word *lovers*). "The entire room got up and joined in, including me and Byron," says Jessica. "It was the most moving part of the party for us."

Thou hast no faults, or I no faults can spy;
Thou art all beauty, or all blindness I.

—*Anonymous*

Here's to my mother-in-law's daughter,
Here's to her father-in-law's son;
And here's to the vows we've just taken,
And the life we've just begun.

—*Traditional toast*

But here's the joy; my friend and I are one . . .
Then she loves but me alone!

—*William Shakespeare, Sonnet 42*

To my wife,
My bride and joy.

— *Anonymous*

Here's to you who halves my sorrows and
doubles my joys.

—*Anonymous toast*

From Couple to Parents

All that I am or hope to be, I owe to my
angel mother.

—*Abraham Lincoln*

Oh, the love of a mother, love which
none can forget.

—*Victor Hugo*

A mother is the truest friend we have.

—*Washington Irving*

God could not be everywhere, so he
made mothers.

—*Proverb*

A father is someone you look up to no
matter how tall you grow.

—*Anonymous*

Prewedding Party Toasting

At an engagement party   The father of the bride toasts the couple and formally announces their engagement to those gathered. Other relatives and friends may say something, as well.

At a shower   A toast is not traditionally part of this party, but close relatives and friends should feel free to formally share their good wishes for you in front of the other guests. A popular activity at a bridal shower is for the guests to tell funny or touching stories or to share marriage wisdom with the bride.

At bachelor/bachelorette parties   This is where the "raunchier" toasts can be offered, or where the bride's or groom's past romantic life can be mentioned or poked harmless fun at by attendants and friends. Just don't go too far if parents are on hand!

At a rehearsal dinner   If you're inviting out-of-town guests and this event will be rather large, it's a great opportunity for people to toast the couple. The hosts of the party—traditionally the groom's parents—might begin by welcoming the guests and thanking them for traveling to the wedding. Then the best man can start the toasting, and things progress quite similarly as they will at the wedding. If you will only invite your immediate families and the wedding party to the rehearsal dinner, you can eliminate the toasting or simply do it very casually.

To father—
Directly after God in heaven comes Papa.

—*Wolfgang Amadeus Mozart*

My father has given me the greatest treasure a father can give—a piece of himself.

—*Suzanne Chazin*

From Couple to Guests

May the friends of our youth be the companions of our old age.

—*Traditional toast*

Among those whom I like, I can find no common denominator, but among those whom I love, I can; all of them make me laugh.

—*W. H. Auden*

Here's to Eternity—may we spend it in as
good company as this night finds us.

　　—*Traditional toast*

It is around the table that friends
understand best the warmth of being
together.

　　—*Italian proverb*

Happiness consists not in the multitude of friends
but in their worth and choice.

　　—*Ben Jonson*

May our house always be too small to
hold all our friends.

　　—*Myrtle Reed*

To friendship: The only cement that will
hold the world together.

　　—*Traditional toast*

Absent friends—though out of sight we
recognize them with our glasses.

　　—*Anonymous toast*

**For more information on toasting or to submit a toast,
visit www.theknot.com/toasts**

NOTES

Speeches
and Toasts

source biographies

Here are a few words about each of the writers featured in the Readings section. For information on those we've quoted in Programs and Toasts, try www.biography.com or www.brittanica.com.

DANTE ALIGHIERI (1265–1321) was an Italian poet who is well known by just his first name as the author of *The Divine Comedy: Inferno, Purgatory, and Paradise,* one of the great masterpieces of world literature.

YEHUDA AMICHAI (b. 1924) immigrated to Israel from Germany in 1936 and is considered Israel's most important poet. He has published eleven volumes of poetry in Hebrew, two novels, and a book of short stories. His work has been translated into more than thirty languages.

CHARLOTTE BRONTË (1816–1855) wrote four novels during the Victorian era, the most famous of which is *Jane Eyre.*

EMILY BRONTË (1818–1848), Charlotte's slightly younger sister (they had another writer sibling, Anne), wrote poetry in addition to her intense, passionate, much-loved novel *Wuthering Heights.* All her work displays her preoccuptation with love and death.

ELIZABETH BARRETT BROWNING (1806–1861) was married to the poet Robert Browning, and her feelings for him inspired her love poetry. In fact, *Sonnets from the Portuguese* details her love affair with Robert.

ROBERT BURNS (1759–1796) was a Scottish poet known for his satire and wit. He set many verses to old Scottish tunes.

LEO BUSCAGLIA (1924–1998), a renowned lecturer and professor at the University of Southern California, he was the author of such books as *Living, Loving and Learning* and *Born for Love* and a tireless advocate of the power of love, promoting the creation of loving relationships and the pursuit of happiness.

WILLIAM CAVENDISH (1593–1676) was a Duke of Newcastle, England, who in addition to poetry wrote plays and songs.

E. E. CUMMINGS (1894–1962) is best known for his all-lowercase poetic style and the fun he had with punctuation and spacing. He wrote many deeply emotional poems filled with sensual imagery and often touched with gentle humor.

LOUIS DE BERNIERES (b. 1954) is a prize-winning British author who has published a trilogy of tragicomic novels: *The War of Don Emmanuel's Nether Parts, Señor Vivo and the Coca Lord,* and *The Troublesome Children of Cardinal Guzman.*

ANTOINE DE SAINT-EXUPÉRY (1900–1944) was a French author whose writings have been translated into hundreds of languages. *The Little Prince* still sells 135,000 copies a year in the United States, over fifty years after it was written.

JOHN DONNE (1572–1631) is known for his passionate, metaphysical poetry. Besides "A Valediction: Forbidding Mourning," his most famous poems include "The Good-Morrow" and the Holy Sonnet that begins "Death be not proud." His work served as an important motif in the recent play *Wit*.

MICHAEL DRAYTON (1563–1631) was an Elizabethan poet who wrote much about love and heroism. He is known for the nationalistic ode "His Ballad of Agincourt" and the end-of-love poem "Since There's No Help."

RALPH WALDO EMERSON (1803–1882) was an American philosopher, essayist, and lecturer in addition to poet. He was a Unitarian minister for a time before he became interested in transcendentalism, which drew upon the teachings of Hinduism, among other philosophies.

ARTHUR DAVISON FICKE (1883–1945) was an American poet. In 1916 he, along with two friends, concocted a fanciful group of experimental poets called the "Spectric" school. In addition to his poetry, Ficke's interepretation of Japanese painting enjoyed an international reputation.

KAHLIL GIBRAN (1883–1931) was a Lebanese poet and novelist who wrote in both English and Arabic; he lived for a time in New York. Fusing elements of Eastern and Western mysticism, he created the very well-known (and oft-read at weddings) book, *The Prophet.*

NIKKI GIOVANNI (b. 1943) is an African-American poet, the author of *Racism 101* and more than fourteen volumes of poetry.

LOUISE GLÜCK (b. 1943) is an American poet. Her book *The Wild Iris,* from which "The White Lilies" is taken, won the Pulitzer Prize for Poetry in 1993.

GUIDO GUINIZELLI (c. 1230–1276) was an Italian poet and jurist from Bologna who moved beyond the Provençal conception of courtly love (the sonnet is said to have originated in Sicily) to a more mystical, spiritual, and philosophical interpretation. Guinizelli's work inspired Dante Alighieri himself, who called him his literary father.

SEAMUS HEANEY (b. 1939) is an Irish poet who writes frequently about his homeland—from early naturalist work to contemporary Ireland, and most recently about his own exile. He won the Nobel Prize for Literature in 1995.

D. H. LAWRENCE (1885–1930) was a teacher before turning to poetry. He is known for his intimate style—his poems seem to speak directly to a "you." He is also famous for the groundbreaking novels *Women in Love* and *Lady Chatterley's Lover.*

CHRISTOPHER MARLOWE (1564–1593) wrote poetry and plays; it was said he was often imitated by Shakespeare early on. One controversial speculation holds that Marlowe faked an early death and took up a new identity—as William Shakespeare! One of his most famous works is his play *Doctor Faustus.*

JANET MILES's poem "Two Trees" is included in the book *Images of Women in Transition* (Saint Mary's Press, 1991).

JOHN MILTON (1608–1674), was an English writer famous for writing the incredible epic poem *Paradise Lost,* excerpted here, as well as *Paradise*

Regained. Earlier in his life he had written many controversial religious pamphlets.

THOMAS MOORE (1779–1852) was an Irish poet and patriot probably best known for his *Irish Melodies,* a group of lyrics set to music (one of which is the poem published here, "Believe Me If All Those Endearing Young Charms"). He was a friend of Lord Byron and published a notable biography of him.

WILLIAM MORRIS (1834–1896), an English poet, early on became a member of painter-poet Dante Gabriel Rossetti's Pre-Raphaelite movement. He wrote many historical, epic poems, and eventually became involved in the Socialist movement, which he wrote about widely.

OGDEN NASH (1902–1971) was an American poet and humorist who wrote a wide range of verse that's highly comical, often absurd, and always quotable.

PABLO NERUDA (1904–1973) was a Chilean poet, diplomat, and Communist leader who wrote surreal, highly personal, and sensual verse. He won the Nobel Prize for Literature in 1971, and he was rendered as a likable, romantic character in the 1995 movie *Il Postino.*

KENNETH PATCHEN (1911–1972) was an American poet and novelist known for his free-form verse and wide-ranging subject matter, from satire to metaphysical love poetry. He often illustrated his books with his own drawings.

MARGE PIERCY (b. 1936) is an American poet and novelist and one of the best-selling poets in the United States today. Her work often addresses issues of Judaism, feminism, and ecology.

WINTHROP MACKWORTH PRAED (1802–1839) was an English poet and essayist, a Conservative member of Parliament, and even a political satirist, but he is remembered best for his graceful, light verse.

KENNETH REXROTH (1905–1982) was an American poet, critic, and translator associated with the Beat writers and poets in San Francisco. He translated much Asian poetry, including "Married Love" by Kuan Tao-Shêng, which appears in this book. He also wrote a book of verse plays and several books of essays.

RAINER MARIA RILKE (1875–1926) was born in Prague and lived and wrote his passionate, insightful poetry and prose in Munich. The most famous are probably *Letters to a Young Poet* and the *Duino Elegies.* STEPHEN MITCHELL has translated much of Rilke's work, among other poets and writers.

CHRISTINA ROSSETTI (1830–1894), a British poet, was seen by many as an early feminist, constantly trying to reconcile her own conflicting views about religion, ambition, familial obligation, and Victorian ideals of what a woman should be. She wrote introspective, emotional poetry about love. Her brother Dante Gabriel Rossetti was also a poet.

RUMI (1207–1273) was a Persian poet and mystic. His major work is the *Mathnawi,* a vast work of spiritual teaching in incredibly beautiful and lyric stories and poetry. It is one of the enduring treasures of the Persian-speaking world. He wrote the poem "This Marriage" for his son's wedding. COLEMAN BARKS is one of the foremost Rumi translators.

BERTRAND RUSSELL (1872–1970) was a British philosopher, mathematician, and social reformer who won the Nobel Prize for Literature in 1950.

WILLIAM SHAKESPEARE (1564–1616) is considered the most famous and influential playwright ever. Among his many histories, comedies, and tragedies, plays like *Romeo and Juliet, Hamlet, King Lear, Othello, Macbeth,* and *A Midsummer Night's Dream* are some of the most read and well known. He also wrote poetry, including 154 sonnets (several of which are included in this book); the sonnets are by far his most important non-dramatic verse.

SIR PHILIP SIDNEY (1554–1586) was one of the most important, innovative figures of the sixteenth-century English Renaissance, along with Shakespeare and Edmund Spenser. His best-known work is the sonnet sequence *Astrophel and Stella.*

ALGERNON CHARLES SWINBURNE (1837–1909), an English poet, wrote sensual poetry and also loved Greek mythology and classical verse. He was a close friend of painter-poet Dante Gabriel Rossetti and part of his Pre-Raphaelite group of artists and poets. Swinburne championed unorthodox political and moral beliefs and poetic tastes.

SARA TEASDALE (1884–1933) wrote lyrical and highly personal poetry. Her book *Love Songs* won the Pulitzer Prize for Poetry in 1918. She was quite reclusive and, unfortunately, died by her own hand at the age of forty-eight.

KUAN TAO-SHÊNG (1262–1319), also known as Madame Kuan, was the wife of Chao-Meng-fu, a noted Chinese painter and calligrapher; besides being a poet, she also painted and did calligraphy herself.

LAU TZU (sixth century B.C.), a philosopher and poet of ancient China, wrote the Tao Te Ching and is considered the founder of Taoism. He was supposedly appointed head librarian of the imperial archives at Lu-oyang, where he immersed himself in the study of history, philosophy, and literature. Confucius visited with him and was in awe of his intellect. When Lau Tzu decided to leave civilization behind and departed Lu-oyang, a guard at the gate asked him to write down his thoughts on the Tao for posterity. Lau Tzu agreed, and the work came to be known as the Tao Te Ching. WILLIAM MARTIN has studied the Tao for a decade and is the author of *The Parent's Tao Te Ching* and *The Couple's Tao Te Ching*.

WALT WHITMAN (1819–1892) was the most influential American poet of his time. He worked as a journalist in and around New York City before turning to poetry—his first effort was the daring book *Leaves of Grass*.

resources

Officiants/Vows

Bill Swetmon, ordained nondenominational minister:
http://members.aol.com/BSwetmon/wed.html

Joyce Gioia, multifaith clergywoman:
(800) 879-7475
http://www.weddingcircle.com/gioia/

Joan Hawxhurst, founding editor of Dovetail Publishing,
and her book, *Interfaith Wedding Ceremonies: Samples and Sources.*
(Dovetail Publishing, 1996)
http://www.mich.com/~dovetail/

The Reverends Irwin and Florence Schnurman:
(631) 345-3606
http://www.interfaithministers.com/union.htm

Dr. Tino Ballesteros, Minister of Christian education
at The Crystal Cathedral:
(714) 971-4041

Music

DJ

Steve McEwen, FM Entertainment, Chicago
(773) 695-9985
http://www.fment.com/

Bands

Reid Spears, Inside Out, Streamwood, Illinois
(630) 837-6833
InsdOutRS@aol.com

Ted Knight, A Little Knight Music, South Florida
(561) 498-8866
http://www.tedknight.com/

permissions

I gratefully acknowledge the following sources, which are included in this book. They are listed alphabetically by author's last name.

Yehuda Amichai: "Both Together and Each Apart" by Yehuda Amichai from *Yehuda Amichai: A Life of Poetry 1948–1994* by Yehuda Amichai. Copyright © 1994 by HarperCollins Publishers, Inc. Hebrew-language version copyright © 1994 by Yehuda Amichai. Reprinted by permission of HarperCollins Publishers, Inc.

Yehuda Amichai: "I Sat in the Happiness" by Yehuda Amichai from *Yehuda Amichai: A Life of Poetry 1948–1994* by Yehuda Amichai. Copyright © 1994 by HarperCollins Publishers, Inc. Hebrew-language version copyright © 1994 by Yehuda Amichai. Reprinted by permission of HarperCollins Publishers, Inc.

E. E. Cummings: "somewhere i have never travelled,gladly beyond" by E. E. Cummings. Copyright 1931, © 1959, 1991 by the Trustees for the E. E. Cummings Trust. Copyright © 1979 by George James Firmage, from *Complete Poems: 1904–1962* by E. E. Cummings, edited by George J. Firmage. Used by permission of Liveright Publishing Corporation.

John Egerton: "Cool breeze" by John Egerton. Copyright © 1990 by John Egerton. Reprinted by permission of John Egerton.

Arthur Davison Ficke: "The Sonnet" by Arthur Davison Ficke is from *Voices,* Summer 1945, and is reprinted in *A Humanist Wedding Service* by Corliss Lamont, copyrighted © 1972, Prometheus Books.

Kahlil Gibran: Excerpt from *The Prophet* by Kahlil Gibran. Copyright © 1923 by Kahlil Gibran and renewed 1951 by Administrators C T A of Kahlil Gibran estate and Mary G. Gibran. Reprinted by permission of Alfred A. Knopf, a Division of Random House, Inc.

Nikki Giovanni: "Love Is" from *Love Poems* by Nikki Giovanni. Copyright © 1968–1997 by Nikki Giovanni. Reprinted by permission of HarperCollins Publishers, Inc. William Morrow & Company, Inc.

————. "And I Have You" from *Love Poems* by Nikki Giovanni. Copyright © 1968–1997 by Nikki Giovanni. Reprinted by permission of HarperCollins Publishers, Inc. William Morrow & Company, Inc.

————. Excerpt from "Resignation" from *Love Poems* by Nikki Giovanni. Copyright © 1968–1997 by Nikki Giovanni. Reprinted by permission of HarperCollins Publishers, Inc. William Morrow & Company, Inc.

————. "You Came, Too" from *Love Poems* by Nikki Giovanni. Copyright © 1968–1997 by Nikki Giovanni. Reprinted by permission of HarperCollins Publishers Inc. William Morrow & Company Inc.

Louis Glück: "The White Lilies" by Louise Glück from *The Wild Iris* by Louise Glück. Copyright © 1993 by Louise Glück. Reprinted by permission of HarperCollins Publishers, Inc.

Mihri Hatun: Excerpt from "At one glance . . ." translated by Talat S. Halman from *The Penguin Book of Women Poets,* edited by Carol Cosman, Joan Keefe, and Kathleen Weaver. Copyright © 1978 by Carol Cosman, Joan Keefe, and Kathleen Weaver. Reprinted by permission of Talat S. Halman.

Seamus Heaney: "Scaffolding" by Seamus Heaney from *POEMS 1965–1975* by Seamus Heaney. Copyright © 1980 by Seamus Heaney. Reprinted by permission of Farrar, Straus and Giroux, LLC.

D. H. Lawrence: Excerpt from "Know Deeply, Know Thyself More Deeply" by D. H. Lawrence, from *The Complete Poems of D. H. Lawrence* by D. H. Lawrence, edited by V. de Sola Pinto & F. W. Roberts, copyright © 1964, 1971 by Angelo Ravagli and C. M. Weekley, Executors of the Estate of Frieda Lawrence Ravagli. Used by permission of Viking Penguin, a division of Penguin Putnam Inc.

———. "In Love That Long" by Rumi, translated by Coleman Barks from *The Glance: Songs of Soul-Meeting* (Viking, 1999). Reprinted by permission of Coleman Barks.

Scripture excerpts are taken from the New American Bible. Copyright © 1970. Confraternity of Christian Doctrine, Inc., Washington, D.C. Used with permission. All rights reserved. No part of the *New American Bible* may be reproduced by any means without permission in writing from the copyright owner.

Kuan Tao-shêng: "Married Love, by Kuan Tao-shêng," translated by Kenneth Rexroth, from *Women Poets of China*. Copyright © 1973 by Kenneth Rexroth and Ling Chung. Reprinted by permission of New Direction Publishing Corp.

Vidyapati, Hindu love poem from *In Praise of Krishna*, by E. C. Dimock and D. Levertov. Reprinted with the permission of The Asia Society.

Here is a list of our additional sources for the book:

101 Classic Love Poems. Chicago: NTC/Contemporary Publishing Group, 1988.

Ackerman, Diane, and Jeanne Mackin, eds. *The Book of Love.* New York: W. W. Norton & Company, 1998.

Alighieri, Dante. *The Divine Comedy: Inferno, Purgatorio, Paradiso.* Translated by Allen Mandelbaum. New York: Alfred A. Knopf, 1995.

Brontë, Charlotte. *Jane Eyre.* New York: Penguin Classics, 1996.

Brontë, Emily. *Wuthering Heights.* New York: Penguin Classics, 1996.

Browning, Elizabeth Barrett. *Sonnets From the Portuguese.* New York: St. Martin's Press, 1986.

Buechner, Frederick. *Magnificent Defeat.* San Francisco: HarperSanFrancisco, 1985.

Buscaglia, Leo. *Love.* New York: Fawcett Columbine, 1996.

Carroll, Jonathan. *Outside the Dog Museum.* New York: Doubleday, 1992.

De Bernières, Louis. *Corelli's Mandolin.* New York: Vintage Books, 1995.

Donne, John. *The Complete English Poems.* New York: Everyman's Library, 1991.

Emerson, Ralph Waldo. *Ralph Waldo Emerson: Selected Poems and Translations.* Edited by Paul Kane and Harold Bloom. New York: Library of America, 1994.

Friedman, Gil, comp. *A Dictionary of Love.* Arcata, CA: Yara Press, 1990.

Fromm, Erich. *The Art of Loving.* New York: HarperCollins Publishers, Inc., 1989.

Gardner, Helen Louise, ed. *The New Oxford Book of English Verse, 1250–1950.* New York: Oxford University Press, Inc., 1972.

Hanh, Thich Nhat. *The Heart of Buddha's Teaching.* New York: Broadway Books, 1999.

Kipfer, Barbara Ann, ed. *Bartlett's Book of Love Quotations.* Boston: Little, Brown and Company, Inc., 1994.

Milton, John. *John Milton's Paradise Lost.* Edited by Harold Bloom. New York: Chelsea House Publishing, 2000.

Nin, Anais. *The Diary of Anaïs Nin 1934–1939.* Edited by Gunther Stuhlmann. San Francisco: Harcourt Brace, 1986.

Proust, Marcel. *Remembrance of Things Past.* Translated by C. K. Scott-Moncrieff and Terence Kilmartin. New York: Random House, 1982.

Ricks, Christopher, ed. *The New Oxford Book of Victorian Verse.* New York: Oxford University Press, 1990.

Rilke, Rainer Maria. *Letters to a Young Poet.* Translated by M. D. Herter Norton. New York: W. W. Norton & Company, 1994.

Roberts, Cokie, and Steve Roberts. *From This Day Forward.* New York: William Morrow & Company, 2000.

Rosenthal, M. L., ed. *Poetry in English: An Anthology.* New York: Oxford University Press, 1987.

Rossetti, Christina Georgina. *Christina Rossetti: Selected Poems.* New York: St. Martin's Press, 1995.

Rossetti, Dante Gabriel. *Selected Poems and Translations.* Manchester, UK: Carcanet Press, 1995.

Russell, Bertrand. *Marriage and Morals.* New York: Liveright Publishing Corporation, 1981.

Saint-Exupéry, Antoine de. *The Little Prince.* Translated by Katherine Woods. San Francisco: Harcourt Brace, 1943.

Shakespeare, William. *The Sonnets: William Shakespeare.* New York: Random House, 1997.

Sidney, Sir Philip. *Sir Philip Sidney: Selected Prose and Poetry.* Edited by Robert Kimbrough. Madison: The University of Wisconsin Press, 1994.

Simon, Raymond, ed. *Love is Enough: Poems and Painting Celebrating Love.* Chicago: NTC/Contemporary Publishing Group, 2000.

University of Virginia, Electronic Text Center, Alderman Library, for Shoshone love poem (etext@Virginia.edu).

Whiston, Lionel A. *For Those in Love.* Nashville: Abingdon Press, 1983.

Whitman, Walt. *Leaves of Grass.* New York: Signet, 2000.

Williamson, Marianne. *Illuminata: Thoughts, Prayers, Rites of Passage.* New York: Random House, 1994.

Woodring, Carl, and James Shapiro, eds. *The Columbia Anthology of British Poetry.* New York: Columbia University Press, 1995.

Yager, Cary, comp. *The Bride's Book of Poems.* Chicago: NTC/Contemporary Publishing, 1995.

photo credits

We gratefully acknowledge the following:

Page ii: Marie Labbancz Photography, www.artoflove.com

Page 2: Elizabeth Grubb Photography, www.elizabethphotography.com

Page 22: Clive Russ, www.cliveruss.com

Pages 28, 113: Angie Silvy Photography, www.angiesilvyphotography.com

Page 76: Ashley Garmon Photographers, http://ccwf.cc.utexas.edu/~carson/AGPhoto/home.html

Page 84: David Max Steinberg and Amy Vanneman, The Lighthouse on Martha's Vineyard, www.vineyardwedding.com

Pages 92, 98: Judy West Photography, www.judywestphotography.com

Page 96: Jeff Greenough Photography, www.jeffgreenough.com

Page 102: David Loeb, Edward Fox Photography, www.edwardfox.com

Page 140: Lynn Spinnato & Jack Roman, Mark Kauffman Photography, www.markkauffman.com

Page 144: Missy McLamb Photographers, www.missymclamb.com

Page 154: Jenny Edwards Photography, www.jenedw.com

Page 174: John Henry Photography, www.maui.net/~jhphoto/

index